MYSTERY SOLVED!

Human Immortality Revealed

SHAHAN SHAMMAS

WORTHWHILE PUBLICATIONS

Copyright © 2021 Shahan Shammas

Copyright ☐ 2021 by Shahan Shammas. All rights reserved. No part of this book may be reproduced or transmitted in any form or by any means, electronic or mechanical, including photocopying, recording, or by an information storage and retrieval system–except by a reviewer who may quote brief passages in a review to be printed in a magazine or newspaper–without permission in writing from the publisher. For information, please contact Worthwhile Publications at shahanshammas@gmail.com

Although the author and publisher have made every effort to ensure the accuracy and completeness of information contained in this book, we assume no responsibility for errors, inaccuracies, omissions, or any inconsistencies herein. Any slights on people, places, or organizations are unintentional.

ISBN-13: 9780966202892
ISBN-10: 0966202899

To my wife, Barbara, and my daughters Olivia and Emily and their husbands Ben and Antony. To the brave souls unafraid to question their beliefs, examine their hearts and Listen to The Voice Within. To anyone ready to be transformed and live to make a positive difference in their lives and the lives of others.

CONTENTS

Title Page
Copyright
Dedication
Preface — 1
Introduction — 3
Part I — 11
"Touching Heaven" — 12
The Spark — 16
Reflection — 19
Dream – The Assembly — 21
Clues about the Nature of My Self — 24
The Value of Experience — 33
Part II — 39
The Miraculous — 40
Why Same Body Immortality Would Never Work — 50
Cyclic Immortality, a Preferred Alternative — 52
Questions to Consider — 63
Part III — 72
What Constitutes Proof? — 73

The Evidence	79
Soul, Fact or Fiction	80
What is Soul?	82
Cyclic Immortality, Fact or Fiction	96
Part IV	113
The Mysteries	114
Birth. Where Do We Come From, If Anywhere? Why Don't We Remember?	117
Why Don't We Remember where we came from?	120
Death. Where Do We Go After We Die, If Anywhere?	124
Does Life Have a Purpose?	131
Why Are We Attracted To Or Repulsed By Certain Individuals?	138
Why Do We Experience Misery, Calamities, Challenge, Pain And Suffering? Why Evil? Is There Justice?	141
7. Why Sacrifice?	153
Where Do Our Ideas, Inspiration, And Sense Of Wonder Come From?	157
Why Do We Dream?	162
When Babies Are Born, Where Do Their Souls Come From? Are There New Souls?	168
The Mystery Of Identity. What Is Self?	171
What Exactly Is The Nature Of God?	175
Who Are We In Relation To God?	177
Part V	179
Making the Most of the Revelation	180

Understand the Nature of Life	181
Make the Most of this Life	185
C. Plan Our Next Life	209
Part VI	219
The Human Experience Revisited	220
Conclusion	230
Note to the reader	234
Acknowledgement	235
About The Author	237
Books By This Author	239

PREFACE

We must make sense of our world, yet mysteries abound. In the absence of knowledge, we rely on belief. Yet, knowledge is possible. The key to finding solutions to the mysteries surrounding us is an open mind, persistent asking, insistent knocking and not giving up. It is only a matter of time for the proper sequence of events to occur and for an answer to appear. I know this is true because this is what happened to me. I asked and I received. My asking was persistent, insistent and demanding.

What I asked for was an answer to the mystery of death – why we die. What I received was a revelation so impactful that it resolved, not only the mysteries of life and death, but also many other mysteries. It answered all of my questions and gave me peace, understanding and satisfaction.

What I have learned is insightful. What I have discovered is profound. Even though we can never impart the wisdom gained from an experience to another, we can share our experiences in the hope that some might benefit from them.

My purpose in writing this book is not to convince or convert anyone. It is to share my greatest revelation. I am offering what I have discovered in the hope that it will help to disclose a truth that has been around since the beginning of time. The implications of this revelation are profound. They impart profound **knowledge** and **understanding**, abiding **peace** and pure **serenity**. Your life can be transformed just as mine was.

All of the experiences in this book are factual. When and where they took place is not as relevant as the fact that they did happen. The value, insights, and knowledge gleaned from them are indispensable.

INTRODUCTION

The Human Experience

> *A lot of people think they should be happy all the time. But the writer understands you need both. You need the whole piano: the richness of the whole human experience. Depression, suffering and anger are all part of being human.* — Janet Fitch

We are surrounded by mysteries. We are born. However, we do not know where we came from, if anywhere. We die, and we do not know where we go, if anywhere. We have religions, but we do not know for sure if there is even a God. We are led to believe that some mysteries are beyond human comprehension. What if this is not true? What if, suddenly, everything made perfect sense? What if we understood the nature of life? What if we found out why we struggle, suffer, age and die? What if we are certain that we have a soul? What if we had an understanding of the role and nature of evil? Would having answers make a difference?

Are we simply highly evolved beasts or is there more to us? Even the Old Testament states that we are mere animals (*Ecclesiastes 3:18-22.*) Yet, in my book **Listening to The Voice Within, becoming enlightened,** I list 12 criteria that unequivocally sets us apart from animals. One of the important distinctions between us and our closest animal relatives, the apes and chimpanzees, is the number of chromosome pairs. While they have 24 pairs of chromosomes, we have 23. Somehow, two small pairs of chromosomes in humans fused together to form a single chromosome. Why did this happen? Was it simply a random mutation?

If we evolved to be what we are, was this evolution haphazard? Was it an accident due to chance alone? I do not believe so. What may appear random initially, turns out not to be so. Evolution is not arbitrary. It is directed toward ever-increasing diversity, efficiency, miniaturization, higher consciousness and better collaboration. We are on the verge of directing the course of our own evolution through conscious intent and freedom of choice.

The "need" for diversification appears to be a predominant "intent" in nature. That is why inbreeding is frowned upon and discouraged, even in animals. In fact, the main reason sex evolved is to ensure diversification. While the vast majority of cells are content to reproduce asexually maintaining their "purity", only egg and sperm cells replicate sexually. Sex cells have single strand chromosomes. They not only cross over, but unite with chromosomes from the other parent, thus, ensuring diversity. Why diversity is important to life will become clear when we read the mystery of cell division later on in this book.

To better understand the nature of the human experience, let us consider a few facts:

- We are born with an expiration date – we live, we age and we die. We have differing life spans. Some live until old age while others die young. Is this fair?

- Each individual has gifts and challenges. While some are intellectuals, others are endowed with natural proclivities. Living affords us a diversity of experiences ranging from painful to pleasurable, from struggle to comfort, from defeat to triumph, and from agony to joy. Many live in abject poverty while a few live in luxurious abundance. Is this purely by chance? Is life unfair governed by the "luck of the draw" or are there hidden forces at play?

- Our memory is selective and fragmented. Even after our nervous system is fully developed, we instinctively dismiss and forget what is not important. A filter is always in place. We retain only the highlights of our lives. How does the brain decide what is important for us? Is survival the only criteria?

- Our understanding is ever increasing. Each generation builds on the achievements of the previous one. As we experience, learn and grow, we progress toward maturity. We have come a long way, yet we remain barbaric in many ways. We are extremely efficient killing machines. Why? Why do we still have wars after millions of years of evolution?

- Even though our bodies are constantly changing, we are always aware of ourselves as unique, individual entities. This awareness is constant, ever present, and rides the waves of change and impermanence. How and why do we maintain our sense of identity?

- We are a link in a vast chain, a thread in the enormous web of life. Yet, we are seldom aware of this. We live as if we are separate entities. Even though we refer to ourselves as individuals, in reality, there is no such thing. We do not have a separate existence. We require food, water and air to survive. These are separate from us. Our bodies exist because of planet Earth. Therefore, true individuality as an independent entity is an illusion. We are a **process** rather than a finished product. We are nothing more than a link in a chain, a thread in a web, or a cell in a body. Is our purpose merely to propagate our species? Why aren't we more aware of our interconnectedness? If we were, would we cooperate more and kill less?

- Since the body is subject to disease, aging and death, evolution of the physical body cannot be the ultimate purpose of life. Our physical bodies are not at the top of physical evolution. It is evident that many of us depend on medications to make it through old age. Examining our physical faculties, we notice that we have given up many of our physical acuities as we have evolved mentally. Animals are far better when it comes to physical prowess and the senses. Our senses of hearing and smell are worse than even some of our pets and our vision is pathetic compared to many other species. Why have we stopped improving many of our faculties? If we are at the top of the evolutionary scale, how come our faculties are not? Is mental evolution all that matters? Why can't we be the best mentally and physically?

- Our mental, social, and spiritual evolution are indeed highly advanced. It is clear that mentally, we are advancing; socially, we are improving; and spiritually, we are maturing. These are what set us apart and distinguish us from other species. Are these what matter most? Why?

- We do not live to merely survive even though survival is essential. Quality of life matters. We pursue value and meaning. We endeavor to know and understand. We get bored with mere existence. We seek newness, adventure, excitement, and thrill. Even though we continue to display the primitive emotions of anger, hate, prejudice and superiority, it is apparent that we are evolving the higher emotions of empathy, forgiveness, acceptance, love, compassion, and inclusiveness. Are these the trend of our evolution?

- We are social beings. Even though we can survive on our own, we urgently seek others. We require contact and intimacy. We crave touch and connection. Sex plays a major role in our lives because we have an urge to commune, be intimate, and perpetuate life. This is ingrained in us and beyond our control. By having children, we connect the past with the future. We enable the advancement of the species. More importantly, we afford an opportunity for others to be born, live, experience, age and die just as we had these opportunities. Is this all there is to life?

- We remain oblivious to the deeper meaning of many of our experiences. We have no clue as to what an out-of-body experience really is. Many have near-death experiences. We do not know what these are. A few have experienced extra-sensory perception, yet we have no clue what it is. Even dreams baffle us. We pray, but how many of us know for sure who we are praying to, and if our prayers are received and processed?

- We are confined to our limited world. We seldom venture beyond our comfort zone. We view the world through the aperture of a personal camera focused on what we consider to be important at the time. Yet, if we move the camera around, or better yet, if we pull away from the camera altogether, we see an entirely different vista.

- We are blessed beyond measure. Yet, we seldom stop complaining. Being alive is reason enough to rejoice. If we are advanced in age, we should celebrate for many have died young. Some complain that they are single, unmarried, yet forget that not all married couples are happy. Some who are married complain that they have no children, yet forget that every child is a blessing to its parents, but not necessarily to society. There are many criminals out there; they were children once. Instead of focusing on what we lack, we should appreciate what is at hand. Perhaps we will stop complaining about lacking shoes when we meet someone without feet or legs, as the saying goes.

- I, like many, have been inspired on many occasions. Yet, who knows where inspiration comes from? Why do songs, music, the arts and beauty touch our souls? Why do our spirits soar when we are in love?

- How do we explain prodigies?

- How can we reconcile the belief in God with accidents and natural disasters that cause the death of thousands of innocent people? How can we explain incredible human atrocities such as genocides?

Faced with the vastness of being, a plethora of destructive natural forces and an abundance of mysteries, it is easy to feel insignificant. This is one view. Alone, we are weak indeed. As part of the whole, however, we are powerful, capable and resourceful. We can solve our problems, resolve the mysteries and live abundantly.

No individual needs to be alone unless they choose to. We stand on the shoulders of those who preceded us. We, in turn, can be the shoulders for those who will follow us. Together, we can solve all problems, overcome our challenges and unveil the mysteries.

I learned a great deal from others. Now is the time for me to give back. I want to contribute to those who want to benefit from my experiences. I was enabled. It is time to empower others. There is no limit to how much we can learn and do together. The solution to the riddles of life is at hand. I present to you **my greatest revelation ever.**

PART I

The Search

"TOUCHING HEAVEN"

To see a world in a grain of sand and heaven in a wild flower.
Hold infinity in the palm of your hand and eternity in an hour. — *William Blake*

So far, there have been three times when I "Touched Heaven" and twice when I tasted Soma, the elixir of the gods. "Touching Heaven" is being transfigured. We are no longer our normal selves. It is when we feel so expansive, light and energetic that while walking, we do not feel the ground beneath us. We literally float off the ground. "Touching Heaven" is a gift. It cannot be induced or sought. It is all-encompassing, lasting up to an hour. The one involved touches a different reality, a transcendent reality, that is a privilege to experience.

Tasting Soma, on the other hand, is different. It forms in the mouth of two lovers who are intensely in a loving embrace sharing their essences. There are no indications as to when or if this will happen, but when it does, it is unforgettable. One must experience it to know what it is.

The first time I "Touched Heaven" was in June 1976. I had been dating my future wife since April 16, 1976. I had known that she was going to be my wife, but she was resisting. Barbara lived in Arlington, VA while I lived in Glen Burnie, MD.

John, my best friend in those days, was an Army Chaplain stationed at Ft. Belvoir, VA. He was dating his future wife as well so John and I would double date. On this particular night, after going to the movies, I drove Barbara to Arlington to drop her off. We stood outside of my car and talked for a very long time. Since it was getting late, I suggested that she allow me to spend the night in her room. She refused. At the time, she was sharing a three-bedroom apartment with two of her friends from work. I kept trying to convince her that it would be unsafe for me to drive back to Glen Burnie since it was very late and I was tired. She would not relent.

The discussion was not going anywhere. I was persisting and she was resisting. I had promised that I only wanted to sleep and leave early in the morning. She said she only had a single-bed which she did not want to share. I promised her that I would never touch her. She refused. Realizing that it was getting very late and we were not making any progress, I gave her an ultimatum. "If I leave tonight," I said, "this will be the last time you see me." "Either I stay, or we part ways." After a long consideration, she asked me to promise once more that I would stay on my side of the bed. I did and we went upstairs to her room.

I kept my promise. I did not touch her in that tiny bed, not even accidentally.

In the morning, I got up early before her roommates woke up, showered and sneaked out. I was a transformed person. While driving home I felt so light and expansive, that I had to stop the car, get out, and fully appreciate the state I was in. I was in Heaven.

The second time I "Touched Heaven" was when I was in a heated discussion facing three experienced adults all at once. I had taken a preliminary course with an organization that promoted self-development. They were business-oriented, intent on making the most profit from each participant. The introductory course was a come-on. The price was high, but acceptable. The cost of the higher-level courses was exorbitant. The representatives of the organization were insisting that each participant move on to the next level and then to a yet higher level with a great increase in cost. I did not need or want the higher courses. The representatives were insistent and persistent. They arranged a private meeting to persuade me with three of their best graduates attacking me from all angles. I was deflecting and countering each and every argument they presented. It was like ping-pong, one against three highly skilled opponents.

After an hour of relentless attack, they realized there was no way they could convince me to sign up for the higher-level courses. I was in a "zone" completely ready and fully aware of their tactics. They gave up and I walked out. I was in "Heaven" for the second time.

The third time I "Touched Heaven" was when I had my greatest revelation, the reason for mortality. I discovered why we age and why we die. Suddenly and completely, the gates to these mysteries flung open. I could peek in, see and understand. My knowing and understanding were complete.

THE SPARK

At times our own light goes out and is rekindled by a spark from another person. Each of us has cause to think with deep gratitude of those who have lighted the flame within us.
― *Albert Schweitzer*

I remember exactly when my inquiry started. From a tender age, I had many questions with hardly any answers. My mind was active but my environment was not conducive for answers to the questions I had. The children my age did not show any interest in the subjects that interested me. Neither did the adults. My parent's reply was always the same: "It is the will of God." For them everything was an act of God. But my Uncle Jacob was different; he was curious. I clearly remember him handing me the Bible one day and asking me to read a passage. I could not have been more than nine or ten years old. He pretended to be testing my ability to read, but he made sure that everyone in the room heard the passage I read. To this day I am not certain if he wanted me to read that passage just to test my ability to read, to bring the meaning of the passage to my attention, or simply to make everyone else aware of the passage. Whatever the reason, I never forgot what I read.

> *I said in my heart with regard to the sons of men that God is testing them to show them that they are but beasts. For the fate of the sons of men and the fate of beasts is the same; as one dies, so dies the other. They all have the same breath, and man has no advantage over the beasts; for all is vanity. All go to one place; all are from the dust, and all turn to dust again. Who knows whether the spirit of man goes upward and the spirit of the beast goes down to the earth? So I saw that there is nothing better than that a man should enjoy his work, for that is his lot; who can bring him to see what will be after him?*   Eccl. 3:18-22

The above passage has haunted me ever since I first read it. It was the moment of "conception" of my search. How did my uncle find this particular passage? No one in my family, or anyone else I knew of, read the Bible. We merely went to church and listened to the Bible being read to us. This passage was the trigger that ignited my desire to know and understand. I have never stopped wondering about the mysteries of life and death ever since. This passage did not seem to have an impact on anyone other than myself. My young mind could not accept that I was just as the beasts were and that I had no advantage over them. I knew that I was more, much more. Could the beasts think, talk, read, write, question and wonder? Could they go to school like I did? Does this mean that I have a different type of "breath" from the animals? I could not say. I reasoned that since I was endowed with these extra abilities, they are not for naught. I must be different.

But how exactly was I different? I resolved to find out.

I did not have to wait long for my first clue that there is more to life than what is apparent. It soon became clear to me that what appears obvious is merely at the surface. Life is like a giant iceberg. The portion we see is the part above the water. Life is more than what we see. Just like the iceberg, life has depth. How deep is life? IT IS AS DEEP AS WE WANT IT TO BE! We see based on what we focus on. This, however, does not mean that there is nothing else to see. Life is like a mirror. We shine on life and life reflects back to us what we throw at it. We are the observers while life is the observed. Yet what we see out there is based on who we are as observers. Obviously, animals see differently than we do. Not only that, each of us sees and experiences reality individually and uniquely.

REFLECTION

Without reflection, we go blindly on our way, creating more unintended consequences, and failing to achieve anything useful. – Margaret Wheatley

We had no air conditioning. On hot summer nights, we slept on mats outside in the open yard. I can still remember one particular night. It was soon after my uncle had me read that passage. I could not sleep. The night sky was incredibly bright and clear, full of stars. It invited speculation. I saw several comets, meteorites and a few shooting stars. I kept looking at the sky and wondering about the vastness of space. I began to question the nature of the stars – how far away and how large they were. I wondered if, perhaps, there was an intelligent life form out there somewhere, laying on their ground, looking up at the vast sky and wondering about the same issues I was thinking about. I became aware of my vast ignorance; I knew so little. I wondered if I would ever know and understand to my satisfaction. How can I know what I want to know when there is so much to learn and so little time? Most live less than a century. How can we solve the riddles around us with such a brief life span? One thought was evident to me. Even though it is easy to feel insignificant in the face of the vastness of being, I did not feel insignificant. I knew, deep within, that my life did matter and that somehow, I was relevant.

Soon my thoughts returned to my current reality. How did I end up here born into this particular family? Did I really want to be born from parents who could barely read or write? Did I want to be the second child of a six-child family? Did I choose to be born as a male? Why? And if I did, why did I choose Aleppo, Syria of all the places to be born? And what about the day and time of my birth, or even the historic time in which I was born. Did I choose these as well? Was all of this by choice or was it all by chance and coincidence?

As far as I know, my parents had their children by chance and due to circumstance. No one practiced birth control. No one had heard of family planning. Most lived in blissful ignorance. My father believed that it was up to him to have children and it was up to God to care for them. Would I still have been born if my father had a different belief system? Is there a higher intelligence that supervises and manages all? And if there is, how free are we?

I was in deep thought as I lay there in the yard observing the night sky. I do not remember when I finally fell asleep. My thoughts must have had a profound impact on me for that night I had a memorable dream.

DREAM – THE ASSEMBLY

To accomplish great things, we must not only act, but also dream; not only plan, but also believe.
— Anatole Ferance

In this dream I found myself in a meeting "place" in the presence of a group of beings. The setting was like a courtroom. However, there were no judges present, only elders. I refer to the place and the setting as "The Assembly."

I do not know how long I had been in "The Assembly." Initially, I was intensely aware of the elders and the other beings. Soon, I lost track of everyone. I wondered why I was there and what I was supposed to do. I became "restless" and eager to do something, but did not know exactly what to do. I was full of desires yet none were overarching. Somehow, I knew that I had to act. But do what? Suddenly, I "remembered" that I could seek help from the Elders. That is when one of the Elders approached me.

"We are here to assist you achieve all that you decide upon. All you have to do is tell us what you want, but you must submit your request in writing."

When I thought to myself that I had nothing to write on or with, the answer instantly "appeared" in my consciousness. I was to write my thoughts on the screen of my mind leaving indelible marks on my consciousness. The Elder had access to my consciousness, or more accurately, we shared the same consciousness.

What should I ask for? How can I decide what I want? Instantly I heard a voice deep within me: "You want to know the nature of your journey. You want to understand the circumstances under which you were born and what you want to do with your life. You want to know what is the purpose of living. You want to know why you age and die. You want to know if death is the end of it all." I felt overwhelmed, but elated. **I intended in my heart – I want to know, I want to understand, I want answers.**

The Elder looked at me pleased. "And answers you shall have." "However, you must discover them yourself for you are endowed with a trinity of powerful tools. You have a creative mind, a knowing heart and a Higher Self. You optimize these when you learn to use your freedom of choice effectively. With these, you can arrive at the answers you seek. Your experiences will be your guides." As the master Jesus had taught:

> *"Ask and it will be given to you; seek and you will find; knock and the door will be opened for you. For everyone who asks receives, and the one who seeks finds, and to the one who knocks, the door will be opened."* Matt 7:7-8

"But how?", I asked.

"Your life is a series of experiences. Each experience is like a pliable brick that you lay in building the cathedral of your life. It is also a piece of the puzzle that adds to the emerging answers to the questions you pose. The purpose of your life is to live, to experience, to learn, to grow, to find the answers you seek. Then, you must share them with others. When the questions you ask are personally meaningful, it makes life challenging and worthwhile. What you seek must be specific and well defined. The questions must be precise. You must decide which door to knock. Your Higher Self will create the synchronicities you need. It whispers to you as intuition, inspiration and as The Voice Within. Finding answers to your questions is the purpose of your current life. With a clear intent in your heart, you can accomplish anything and achieve whatever you set your mind and heart to if what you seek is personally gratifying."

"The questions you present to us, are also presented to your Higher Self simultaneously. You will be attracted to specific places and circumstances where special experiences will lead you to the answers you seek. Your life is about you. You live to create your unique self. By being born, you place yourself on the stage of life. You are the actor, the producer, and the director on the stage of your life. You are creating and living a drama. Live it as well as you can. Your life can be mediocre or a work of art. Since you have a choice, why not make it a masterpiece? Go for it. Use your freedom of choice. Always clarify and focus on your intentions. They are the lighthouse that will guide you to your safe harbor. Finally, listen to The Voice Within and act on its promptings."

◆ ◆ ◆

CLUES ABOUT THE NATURE OF MY SELF

To thine own self be true, and it must follow, as the night the day, thou canst not then be false to any man.   *– William Shakespeare*

The first clue about the unusual nature of reality was an experience I had that restored some of the serenity I lost when my uncle had me read that passage from the Bible. I soon discovered that I **was** more than dust or beast. There **is** more to me than what is apparent. I am like an ocean. To experience my depth, I must delve within and touch my core. One experience led to another and another. Each was like a piece of a puzzle. When I put them together in their proper "position", a complete picture emerged. I could see clearly. I started to understand and began to receive the answers I was seeking.

First Experience

Out Of The Body

We changed our residence often when I was young, moving from one rental to another. At the time of this experience, I must have been close to five years old. I had just started going to school. We were living in a rental unit near the edge of a small Christian community in Aleppo, Syria that we shared with two other families. One family was Armenian with grown up children who lived elsewhere; the other family was Syriac. The Syriac man, Samaan (Simon), was the caretaker of our church. His son and I went to the same school. Each family had its own bedroom and kitchen. Everyone shared the same water faucet and bathroom which were outside in the courtyard.

One day, when I came back from school, my mother was not home. I looked for her for what seemed like a long time but could not find her. I was getting frustrated and very hungry. I had to do something. I saw that the kitchen door had the key in it, a large iron key about five inches long that I could barely reach. I was too short to turn it and unlock the door. Finally, I managed to turn the key and the kitchen door opened. I went in and started to look for something to eat. We did not have any of the modern conveniences such as a refrigerator or stove. I looked over the counter. I did not find anything that I knew was food, yet I was hungry. Then I saw a large box sitting on the counter. I did not know what it was. After stepping on a pot, I picked up the box. It was a box of Tide detergent. I reached for it, shook it up to find out what was in it. I wondered if the white granules in the box were edible. I was too hungry to pass up the opportunity to try, so I poured some of it into my palm and started to lick it. I did not eat much because it did not taste good. Immediately, I knew I had done something I should not have. I wanted to wash the taste away so I ran out of the kitchen to the yard. I reached for some water and drank it. Instantly foam began to come out of my mouth. I drank some more water. Soon foam covered my mouth and nose. I panicked and began to move about aimlessly. I did not go very far for I could not breathe. I passed out and fell to the ground.

    I never forgot what I experienced next. The neighbor, the church caretaker's wife, came out and saw my body. She got flustered and started to scream, "The boy is dead, the boy is dead, where is his mother?" I wanted to tell her that I was not dead, but as hard as I tried to speak, no voice came out of my mouth. I could not talk or move any part of my body. My body was stiff on the hard ground. That is when I realized I was not in my body. I was above my body about eight feet, looking down at myself lying there motionless on the ground. I was confused. There I am down there yet here I am up here. What is going on? I do not recall how much time passed. While I was in this state pondering my situation, the lady returned with a bucket of water and poured it on me. The cold water shocked me back into my body. By then the foam must have subsided and I could breathe and move my limbs again.

I never forgot this experience. However, I seldom discussed it with anyone. I had no idea what it was that I experienced. I felt that, perhaps, it had something to do with the basic nature of my being. This experience merely whet my appetite to know more. The desire to know myself and understand life was kindled and has never abated.

◆ ◆ ◆

Second Experience

My Mother's Visit

I was sixteen years old when I entered the monastery of the Syrian Orthodox Church of Antioch in Zahle, Lebanon. Like everyone else, I was given two options – stay celibate and become a monk, or if I wanted to get married later on, I could become a priest. At the monastery, we mostly studied, prayed, and discussed various topics. We ate dinner around 5:30 p.m. at which time, the head of the monastery presented us with a topic to discuss. Afterwards, we had our evening prayers from 6:30 - 7:00 p.m. At 7:30 p.m., we had our normal evening study period until 9:30 p.m. Around 10:00 p.m., we went to bed. On Sundays, we went to the local church and participated in the service. Afterwards, we had the day for ourselves. Usually, we took walks in the mountains.

During the study period one evening, I had a strange feeling. I did not want to study. I felt restless and had a strong urge to go to the bedroom and lay down. I asked if I could be excused. Normally, no exceptions were granted unless one was sick. We had to study until 9:30 p.m. and I always did. This was the first time I asked to leave early. Being a good student helped and I was granted permission to leave and go to bed. Where I slept was a large room with eight beds arranged in two rows. My bed was the first in the second row. I went in, changed, brushed my teeth and got into bed. I was the only person in the room. It was very quiet, unusually still.

Suddenly and unexpectedly, I sensed that my mother was in the room. This was more than a mere feeling. I *knew* that my mother was in the room. I was aware of her presence. I sensed a movement in the room that sounded like the swishing movement of heavy wind. I knew, beyond any doubt, that my mother had come to visit me. I had not been thinking of her or even missing her. I lay very still in my bed. I became intensely aware of her presence. I could not see anything or anyone for it was dark. I could only sense, keenly, that she was in the room with me. My mother, seeming like a dense cloud, came closer to my bed and hovered over me. Soon she was completely covering me. I could feel pressure on me. I kept my eyes closed. Even though I could not see anything, I knew from deep within that she came to comfort and reassure me. She surrounded me for a while, impressed her presence on me, then lifted off and was gone. The sense of her presence was overwhelming. I could not stop thinking of her for a long time afterwards.

When my mother was about to pass away at the age of 36, she called her children one-by-one to say goodbye. I was the only one she did not get to see because I was hiding and would not come out. Finally, with her visit in the monastery, my mother got her chance to bid me farewell. This experience left an indelible mark on me. My mother was alive after all. She could even come and visit.

After studying at the monastery for two years, I quit and went to high school in Sidon, Lebanon where I stayed until I graduated. I then went to college. After four years at the American University of Beirut, I received a Bachelor's degree in Biology and immediately emigrated to the United States of America. Soon afterwards, I joined the U.S. Army and received my U.S. citizenship. After serving in the Army for three years, I was discharged, rented an apartment in Glen Burnie, MD and worked at the US Army's First Medical Laboratory at Fort Meade, MD. It was in this apartment that I had my next unusual experience.

Third Experience

Out Of The Body One More Time

It was a sultry Friday night. After tossing and turning in bed for a while, I finally fell asleep. I was in deep sleep when my alarm went off. I could not believe it. Why would the alarm go off on a Saturday morning? Perhaps, I had forgotten to turn it off when I went to bed the night before. The alarm was very loud and annoying. I wanted to turn it off. I tried to reach over and shut the buzzer off, but could not. I was tangled up in the bed sheet that was completely wrapped around me from tossing and turning. The noise from the alarm was disturbing. I had to turn it off. I struggled to loosen myself from the sheet, but failed. I was trying to not completely wake up while attempting to reach the clock and turn it off, but the sheet wrapped around my body prevented me from reaching the clock. Finally, after some struggle, I did reach the clock. I extended my right index finger and attempted to push the alarm button off. To my utter amazement, my finger simply went through the clock. I was flabbergasted. What is happening? I tried again, and again my finger went through the clock and the alarm would not shut off. This is incredible, I thought to myself. Why can't I shut the alarm off? I was agitated but fully aware. Suddenly, I realized that I was not in my bed any more. I was above the bed. I looked down and there lay my body still wrapped in the white sheet. I was astonished. Realizing that I had experienced this before soon allowed me to relax. I became intensely aware of myself. Here I am floating over my bed in the middle of my efficiency in Glen Burnie, MD. I wondered what I could do with this opportunity.

Instantly I realized that this was my chance to experiment and find out more about my reality. I wondered if I could go wherever I wanted. I decided to try. I did not have a particular place in mind, yet I wanted to go somewhere. Suddenly I found myself in a store that was full of electronic equipment. The room was a storage place for old equipment that required repair. I hovered over the pieces studying them. Soon I realized that there was a "cord" coming out of the back of my head. This cord extended all the way back to my body in my bedroom in Glen Burnie. I focused on the cord. I wanted to know its nature. It extended connecting the forehead of my body in bed to the back of my head in this store.

After a while, I attempted to visit my next-door neighbors and impress upon them my visit. I thought I could check with them the next day to find out if they remembered my visit. They were a young couple that I only knew superficially. I was unsure if I should visit them because of privacy. Besides, I did not know what to do or say. I was running out of options of what else to try. That is when suddenly I snapped back into my body and the experience ended.

I have often thought of the cord connecting my two bodies as the wedding band that symbolically unites two in a holy matrimony. My body, the tangible and my intangible self are "umbilically connected" until death. I reasoned that I will remain alive physically for as long as my two bodies remain connected. Death is a severance between the two. How long can the tangible body and my intangible aspect remain united? What keeps them together and what causes their separation? If we can find out what this cause is, perhaps we can control it. I wanted to know.

◆ ◆ ◆

I never forgot these experiences. They were intense, lucid and palpable and I learned a lot from them. There is a tremendous difference between being in the body and being out of it. The two states are worlds apart. It is clear to see that the laws of nature are appropriate only while in their natural environment. These laws are not as absolute as we tend to think of them. Everything is relative. Time, space, cause and effect have different meanings in the different states. The closest state to being out of the body is the one we experience while sleeping and dreaming.

I am not sure how many different states there are. I do know of at least two distinct states – the tangible world we experience in our wakeful state and the intangible world we experience when we dream or when out of the body. The two states are linked and we function in both of them. I am alive in both states. The individuality that I experience is in fact a duality. I have a body in which I live and function, and an intangible aspect that can separate from the body. I am accustomed to thinking that reality is only what I experience in the body because it is physical and tangible. However, there is another world out there that is equally real – the intangible world. It matters little how aware we are of it for it is, never-the-less, real. It has its own unique qualities. To deny its existence is to deny a major aspect of our being.

THE VALUE OF EXPERIENCE

Nothing is a waste of time if you use the experience wisely.   – Aususte Rodin

Earlier today, I took an antibiotic pill. The instructions were that I should take it with food. I, however, swallowed the pill just before I began eating. In a few minutes, I began to feel nauseated. Soon I was vomiting. I learned my lesson – with food means after you eat some food, not at the start of the meal. There is no teacher like experience.

We are irrevocably linked to our experiences. The stronger the emotional investment in an experience, the more enduring the connection. We leave a part of ourselves in each of our experiences. Perhaps, that is how we remember. The link is always there. It is as if "tiny silver chords" link us to each of our experiences.

The value of an experience is the knowledge, proficiency and insights gained. To appreciate value, we often have to experience its lack first. If we had a family member in the military and this member was overseas in harm's way, and if, after a few years this family member came home safely, how do we greet that person? How does that compare to a family member whom we see and interact with every day? Why the difference?

Once we get used to something, we assume that it will always be there. Not true. When I met my wife, she was 23 years old. She was young, sweet and beautiful. I was youthful, slim, trim, and vigorous. Those days are gone. This is not to say that we lost all those qualities, but that those days are forever gone. The body changes. Our passions subside. Our physical abilities peak and begin to decline. The only constant is change. While we have our youth, we take it for granted. We assume that it is forever. While we have our faculties, we take them for granted. We assume that we will always have them. However, it is only after we no longer can see that we begin to truly appreciate the value of sight.

We live to experience and to create memories. Experience is not only that which we desire to have, but also anything that comes our way including the unpleasant. To face any situation successfully requires not only a mental know how, but also the confidence that comes from previous experiences. Experiences are valuable because they give us the confidence to face any situation. Imagine if you won the Mega Million Lotto prize of over half a billion dollars. What would you do? For the unprepared, a sudden windfall could be ruinous. For the prepared, however, the same gift could positively impact millions of lives.

I believe that we attract the experiences we need. They are the answers to our unuttered prayers. They are how we develop a particular talent or skill, resolve a conflict, or realize a deficiency we need to overcome. I also believe that we will continue to attract similar situations until we gain mastery over them. It is best to be prepared for whatever life may bring our way, particularly challenges and difficulties. We cannot grow without them. If we live preparing for what may come and we are ready when the unexpected happens, then we can make the most of the occasion and direct the course of the event without being devastated. Being prepared is vital. That is why Christ gave us the following parable:

The Parable of the Ten Virgins (Matthew 25:1-13)

> *Then the kingdom of heaven will be like ten virgins who took their lamps and went to meet the bridegroom. Five of them were foolish, and five were wise. For when the foolish took their lamps, they took no oil with them, but the wise took flasks of oil with their lamps. As the bridegroom was delayed, they all became drowsy and slept. But at midnight there was a cry, 'Here is the bridegroom! Come out to meet him.' Then all those virgins rose and trimmed their lamps. And the foolish said to the wise, 'Give us some of your oil, for our lamps are going out.' But the wise answered, saying, 'Since there will not be enough for us and for you, go rather to the dealers and buy for yourselves.' And while they were going to buy, the bridegroom came, and those who were ready went in with him to the marriage feast, and the door was shut. Afterward the other virgins came also, saying, 'Lord, lord, open to us.' But he answered, 'Truly, I say to you, I do not know you.' Watch therefore, for you know neither the day nor the hour.*

When asked what was her secret to success, Janet Yellen, the first female Secretary of the Treasury said:

> "For me, being prepared is the most important thing. Fortify yourself by being as prepared and as knowledgeable as you possibly can. That works to bolster your self-confidence. It certainly does for me. And that is what I do to this day. I do not wing it. I never wing it."

(*The Washington Post*, Sunday, September 5, 2021.)

There is a tremendous difference between a novice and an experienced master. The master has weathered a great deal, faced challenges and learned from them. The master is ready for what life may bring. Diverse experiences lead to growth and maturity. Conversely, immaturity is due to the lack of experience. The ancients associated maturity to ripeness and the concept of "good" and immaturity to being unripe and the concept of "evil". Hence, we live to experience and to become ripe, "good" and mature.

Experiences give rise to beliefs. Beliefs, on the other hand, color or even filter out certain experiences. If we have a world view, then everything must fit neatly into our world view. Inconsistencies are not allowed. Beliefs are the lighthouse that guide our lives. For most, these are habitual, inherited and accepted without evaluation. We mostly accept what we are told and taught. We aim to please. A lot is relegated to fate or placed in the hands of God. Living for most is going through life with blindfolds on. We seem to know what the answers should be. Hence, we go about gathering only the pieces that fit the picture we expect. We constantly filter out the experiences that do not fit what we believe and assume. Since we have an idea as to what we are looking for, we only see those pieces that fit our expectations. Yet, to arrive at unadulterated answers, we must allow for unexpected and unusual experiences. I am fortunate to have had several of these early in life, prior to indoctrination and the forming of beliefs about the nature of reality. I was born to parents who were, for all practical purposes, illiterate. They did not feel that they had much to teach their children, so they did not. I grew up with a relatively open mind. Thus, when I had unusual experiences, I made a mental note and filed them in the "important" category rather than just dismissing them. I would visit these memories once in a while and dwell on them hoping to understand their deeper meaning. When I had my first out-of-body experience, I could barely read. I had no indoctrinated beliefs then. These experiences did not get wiped out of my memory due to disbelief or discredit. I did not encourage or discourage these types of experiences. I simply observed them as they took place, reflected on them privately, and then filed them away for later reference. With these experiences as my foundation, I began to unravel the mysteries of life and death.

It is normal to concede that the answers we seek for the questions we have are unavailable and out of reach. It is also normal to live our lives pretending that we do not care to know the answers to the important questions that face us. Equally, we can ignore the questions altogether and live our lives blindly focusing instead on work, necessities and the pursuit of pleasure. I will not do any of these for I cannot know happiness unless and until I answer the call from within. This call is relentless urging me to seek, to find, to understand, to question until a satisfying answer is arrived at. I never give up until I know.

My insistence upon knowing and the persistence with which I sought answers finally yielded an abundant harvest. The premise was simple. It was what Christ had promised and what the Elder in my dream had emphasized:

> *"Ask and it will be given to you; seek and you will find; knock and the door will be opened for you. For everyone who asks receives, and the one who seeks finds, and to the one who knocks, the door will be opened. Is there anyone among you who, if his son asks for bread, will give him a stone? Or if he asks for a fish, will give him a snake?   Matt 7:7-10*

PART II

The Revelation

THE MIRACULOUS

The invariable mark of wisdom is to see the miraculous in the common.

— Ralph Waldo Emerson

On the surface, life seems ordinary. If we could delve deeper into it, life transforms itself right before our eyes. It becomes extraordinary. We are accustomed to looking at life casually. We do not see what is staring us in the face because we are familiar with it. We get used to things and they become commonplace. This is because habitual living dulls our senses and we become oblivious. We stop paying attention and this is by design. It is easy to be overwhelmed by sensory data. We are not aware of the clothes we wear. A normal person does not think about his or her breathing. We are so used to it that we take it for granted. We actually do not even remember that we are breathing until we stop and notice it. Yet, for a drowning person, a breath is tantamount to life itself.

There is nothing ordinary about life if we take the time to discover it. Have you ever looked at a baby, yours or someone else's? If you casually look at a baby, you do not see much. There is much more to what is in front of you than what is apparent. A baby is one of the wonders of the universe. It is a world unfolding right before your eyes.

I recently looked at a detailed picture of a mosquito. The intricacy of its design is amazing. It is a perfect example of nano technology. With its speck of a brain, it knows how to fly, detect prey, reproduce and multiply and above all, become an irritant and elude capture.

Have you ever "seen" a dandelion? Of course you have. It is the weed that you pluck out of your lawn and throw away. However, if you ever examine a dandelion with "open" eyes, an inquisitive mind, and an appreciative heart, would you still throw it away?

There is nothing ordinary about a dandelion. This "weed" is a miracle of nature. It has an astounding design and a pharmacopeia of benefits that we are oblivious to. Just take a look at and observe its seeds. What an amazing design!

What are seeds anyway?

Seeds are the most ingenious and marvelous packaging of intelligence in the known universe. Seeds house DNA and DNA is a marvel to behold.

Watch out where you are stepping for where you place your sole is indeed holy ground.

Open your eyes and see. There is wonder everywhere.

Open your ears and listen. There is incredible music surrounding us.

Open up to life and begin to live. There is much more to life if we only dig a little. We will discover marvels, wonders and miracles that are invaluable and beyond measure. They are there for us free of charge and are a gift from our true Mother – Earth and our spiritual Father – the Sun.

We are indeed children of the universe.

We are rich beyond measure.

We are fortunate beyond comparison.

We are blessed regardless of merit.

We have been given treasures that do not spoil. They are ours to savor but only if we wake up and begin to appreciate what is in front of us. When we live with our eyes open, our minds curious and inquisitive, and our hearts full of wonder, appreciation and gratitude, we experience the miraculous on a daily basis.

The greatest revelation I ever had was there all along staring me in the face. I only had to open my eyes to see and my heart to know. I did. What a revelation! What a discovery!

How It Happened

As incredible as it may sound, it really happened. I unraveled the secrets of life and death. I untangled the mystery of why we age and why we die. Life did not, however, yield its secrets to me easily or quickly. I had to work persistently and passionately for many years to remove the blinders obstructing my view.

It was no accident that the answer came to me when it did. I have always maintained a passion for knowing. I wanted to know the why, not just the how. I neither placed nor accepted any limitations on my capacity to understand and know. I planted the seeds of wanting to know the secrets of life and death by persistent questioning, quiet contemplation and by studying the subject matter over many years. Until then, all I ended up with were bits and pieces of insights that did not comprise a coherent whole. This time, I had the answer and it made perfect sense.

On this particular day, I was on a lunch break near my work area, outside Walter Reed Army Medical Center in Washington, DC. I was walking alone and completely engrossed in my thoughts when suddenly and unexpectedly, life revealed one of its most coveted secrets to me in a flash. The answer to the riddles of life and death became obvious. It was as if a veil had lifted and I could glimpse into the inner workings of nature. All the pieces of the puzzle fit together and I could see the whole picture. The answer was obvious, simple and elegant.

It is fascinating how profound and beautiful the "right" answer is, once we have it. It explains what used to be a mystery. It clarifies what was complicated. It quells the thirst and it gratifies. I remember as a programmer how hard I would work to solve a problem. Initially, the solution seemed difficult, complicated, and out of reach. But in the end, after I overcame all the hurdles and finished testing the solution, I marveled at the simplicity and beauty of the final product. This revelation felt the same.

As soon as I had the answer, I was in rapture. My body felt light and airy like I was floating. I started to walk faster. I wanted to shout and share my revelation with anyone and everyone but restrained myself for I did not know how to communicate what I had just discovered. It seemed impossible to share what I was experiencing. I "Touched Heaven" for the third time.

Why It Happened

At the time of the revelation, I was writing a book titled: **How to Live for as Long as you Want, even forever**. I was facing several obstacles for which I had no answers. After long hours of attempting to resolve the problems facing me, I was struck with a thought. What would I do if and when I discover how to prolong my life, in the same physical body, for as long as I want, even forever? How would I manage my revelation? I had several challenges to contend with:

1. In what stage of my life would I apply my discovery? Did I want to be young forever? Or, should I wait until old age when I am more mature and then "freeze" my status?
2. If I did not die while everyone else did, how long can I live in one locale before I have to move and avoid suspicion?
3. Who would I share the discovery with? To share my discovery would require several hours of instructions and explanations. What if these people wanted me to share it with their loved ones? Soon everyone would be asking me to share my knowledge. I would have no time for myself and I would have no peace. How will I guard the discovery against unwanted intrusion?
4. What if the terminally ill need the benefit of the discovery? Would I share my knowledge? Is prolonged life desirable in all cases?
5. What if I am not happy with my body? Am I stuck with it forever?
6. Will I get bored? Can I maintain my interest, curiosity and enthusiasm? Will I ever get tired of living?
7. What happens if I have an accident and lose a limb or two?

The Solution

To solve the challenges facing me, I resorted to an ingenious strategy. I assumed that I had already solved the problems facing me. After many days of deep thought and prolonged hours of reflection, I took a break. I stopped thinking about it until one day when I was in deep thought walking outside my work area near Walter Reed Army Medical Center. "How did I do it?", "How did I solve my problems?" were the overarching questions on my mind when lightning struck. Instantly, I had my answers. Serendipity.

Asking, seeking, knocking is a spiritual process that creates a "template" in the image of the questions being asked. The more intense, insistent and persistent the questioning, the more refined this template becomes. Intense, passionate desire for an answer "magnetizes" this template and transforms it into a charged blueprint. Once released from the mind, this blueprint roams the Cosmic Mind gathering the solution needed. When all the elements come together, the blueprint is "coupled" with the solution. At the opportune time, it is presented as an inspiration or an insight. This is exactly what happened to me.

Out of the blue, the answer came to me. It became clear that I was living exactly as a wise immortal would. I was mistaken to assume that there was only one way to be immortal – prolonging my existence in the same body. There is an alternative and superior way where we are born, live, die and repeat this cycle over and over ad infinitum. Cyclic immortality resolves all the challenges I was contending with. Initially, the answer made sense. Over time, the elegance and beauty of this revelation were overwhelming and intoxicating.

The Revelation in a Nutshell

I "Touched Heaven" for the third time when I had my greatest revelation ever. The experience was all encompassing. All the answers became available instantly. It was like a "mini bang" exploding in my mind and taking me on an expansive journey where the answer to every mystery was revealed. In a way, it was comparable to the knowledge I gained when I had my near-death experience. Imagine touching an encyclopedia and gaining all the knowledge contained within it instantly. To explain the details will require a lengthy elaboration. Regardless, here are some insights from that revelation:

1. The revelation is the "perfect" solution to the mysteries and the answer to the questions I had.
2. We have "chosen" a unique form of immortality – cyclic – through rebirth as the appropriate means to exercise our immortality. We deliberately forget our immortality because remembering it hinders us from living full, responsible and meaningful lives.

3. Everything is exactly as it should be. We have chosen this life with its circumstances. While on the other side, we plan. On this side, we execute our plans. We planned the major events of this lifetime before we were born, but chose to forget them upon birth so that we are surprised at our choices and their outcomes. This makes life interesting, challenging, mysterious and memorable. We live our plans and experience their consequences, favorable or not.
4. We are never victims unless that is what we choose to be. We are the masters, directors and choreographers of our lives. We are living as we choose to live, even if it does not seem so.
5. It is our desire to experience physical reality. That is why we choose to be born. Learning, growing and maturing can only take place while we are in a physical body undergoing earthly experiences.
6. Being in space/time, we experience change and are mortal. Once outside of space/time, we do not experience change and we know ourselves as immortals.
7. Death is a choice. We decide to die. This decision is subconscious or even unconscious.
8. Birth, pain, pleasure, youth, vitality, health, disease, aging and death are integral aspects of the human experience.
9. Free will is absolute. We can exercise it at any moment and change the trajectory of our lives.

10. Our intentions are our guides. They influence our conscious and subconscious. They mold our experiences and shape our reality. We can learn something from every situation we face.
11. We are souls. The body is a temporary abode necessary for our experiences.
12. Our soul is multi-dimensional, an integral aspect of the forces that create and shape the universe. This is because our soul is always connected to its spiritual source. We are oblivious to this fact because our focus is on the immediate physical experiences we are undergoing. We are lulled into believing that we are only our ego, the physical body and the lower self. As our soul, we are much more.

Most importantly, I was on the wrong path searching for a same-body immortality – living for as long as we want. It would never work.

WHY SAME BODY IMMORTALITY WOULD NEVER WORK

It is not the end of the physical body that should worry us. Rather, our concern must be to live while we're alive - to release our inner selves from the spiritual death that comes with living behind a facade designed to conform to external definitions of who and what we are. – Elisabeth Kubler-Ross

Being eternal, we would not want to be in the same body forever or even too long. What if we wanted to change what we looked like? How about experiencing what it is like to be the opposite sex, a different race, or a new nationality? With same body immortality we are stuck with what we have. We have no say in what body we end up with. Our opportunities to experience the diversity of life are limited.

Here are more disadvantages to same body immortality:

1. We can never experience a new family, a new spouse, new children, or new challenges in raising a family.
2. Our brains have finite storage. How long

before our minds dull from the continuous accumulation of experiences and their memories? There is no refresh button.
3. Boredom will eventually set in.
4. A person will never be able to experience the effects of one's actions on others. There is no chance for karma to play out. Justice will never be served.
5. If we make a serious mistake, we have to live with it. No chance to redeem ourselves. We have only one chance at opportunities.
6. Life will lose its preciousness since there is no expiration date to living.
7. The incentive to achieve will diminish. We have as long as we want to do whatever we want to do. Postponement, procrastination and weakened incentive will dominate living.
8. Above all, we will have to contend with injuries, deformities and handicaps incurred during the course of living. Since the effects of some injuries are permanent, we will always have these.

CYCLIC IMMORTALITY, A PREFERRED ALTERNATIVE

Surely God would not have created such a being as man, with an ability to grasp the infinite, to exist only for a day! No, no, man was made for immortality. —Abraham Lincoln

What if we want to experience being a great pianist, a great scientist, or a great athlete? We know that it is best to start our training at an early age, preferably as a child. Cyclic immortality avails us the opportunity to do so.

What if we want to learn a difficult language such as Chinese or Arabic? We know that it is best to be born into that culture and start our learning at an early age, preferably as a child. Cyclic immortality avails us the opportunity to do so.

What if we want to experience being a king or queen? We would want to be born into a royal family. What if we want to know what it is like to be filthy rich? How about being homeless, poor, and destitute? With cyclic immortality, we can be born into any circumstance we choose. Cyclic immortality provides us with infinite opportunities. Over time, we can experience anything and everything.

Here are more advantages to cyclic immortality:

1. We start each life cycle in a new body. Why be stuck in the same body forever? What if we are not happy with what we have? What if we are too short, too tall, too skinny, too fat, not beautiful or strong enough?
2. We enter each life with a new family under novel conditions, allowing us to develop new relationships, face new challenges and unique experiences. This makes life exciting and alleviates boredom. What matters most for eternal beings are loss of interest, lack of curiosity and a nonchalant attitude toward living. Hence, a variety of experiences, regardless of their nature, is of the utmost importance. Cyclic immortality makes this possible.
3. Our brains will never dull from the continuous accumulation of experiences and their memories. With the start of each lifecycle, we press the "refresh" button and the slate is wiped clean except for what is incorporated as instinct, character and personality.
4. We never forget the important lessons learned in each lifetime. We carry these over from one life to another as aspects of our character and personality. The value of an experience is never lost.
5. Our growth, learning and maturation can continue indefinitely.

6. We can vanquish boredom and death.
7. We can enjoy exciting new encounters with different people, new spouses and children. We can live in different countries under varying conditions.
8. Over several lifetimes, we get to experience the consequences of our actions. Karma is fulfilled, and justice is served.
9. We start each life oblivious to the fact that we have lived before. This makes our lives precious for we are born with an expiration date.
10. By making each life terminal with a fixed duration, we have the impetus and the incentive to accomplish the most within the allotted time.
11. Cyclic immortality explains why we age, why our faculties atrophy and why we suffer. These prepare us for our exit.
12. By having lived in various bodies, in different countries, and in diverse cultures, we become broadminded, tolerant and compassionate. We also have the opportunity to appreciate our planet even more.

It is difficult to imagine that such an ingenious strategy to perpetuate our existence via cyclic immortality can be true. Once we realize that we are consciousness, and that our soul is an inseparable aspect of the creative forces that shape the universe, then it is easy to accept that such a plan is operational. The creativity of consciousness is unlimited. It is the force behind our creative genius and the driving force behind life and evolution. We do not live, age and die because we are victims of circumstance. Death is not a deficiency of nature. It is not a usurper. We choose to age and die, subconsciously or even unconsciously. We live and die because it is our intention to do so and is according to our plan. As we live, die and live again, we sculpt and mold ourselves into beautiful beings.

◆ ◆ ◆

Elegance of Cyclic Immortality

If we want to understand the cyclic nature of existence, all we have to do is look at nature. Water goes through cycles. So do many processes, chemicals and elements such as nitrogen, carbon dioxide, and respiration. In 2021, we witnessed the cyclic emergence of the cicadas. Seasons are cyclic. Calendars are cyclic. Our lives are cyclic as well. We go to sleep every night, dream and then we wake up. We are born, live, grow up, age and die. This cycle repeats itself through our children and their children. Life continues in cycles.

There are various stages in each life cycle. These are obvious when the caterpillar turns into a butterfly. Similarly, in each life cycle, our bodies go through a series of stages as well. We do not simply grow, we unfold. If we watch the human body in time-lapse photography speeded up thousands of times, we clearly see the various stages the body goes through. Birth and childhood are distinct stages associated with dependence. As we approach adolescence, the body goes through a growth spurt. The sexual organs begin to mature along with bodily signs of sexual maturity. Pubic hair, breast enlargement and rounded hips become evident in women; pubic, facial, underarm and chest hair make their appearance in men. As men grow older, nose and ear hair appear and the eyebrows thicken. At old age, the hormones decrease along with sexual desire. Women go through menopause and so do men, although differently. These changes take place regardless of nutrition or exercise. The body is programmed to go through these changes via a biological clock. As these changes occur, our outlook toward life changes and we experience people and the world differently.

If we view living as a wave, we will have a more complete understanding of the cyclic nature of being. A wave cycle consists of two parts: a bell curve above the horizontal line with a crest and another below it with a trough forming a mirror image of the other. Just as one day is night and day, a wave is the seen curve above and the unseen curve below.

> *God called the light Day, and the darkness he called Night. And there was evening and there was morning, the first day.*   Gen 1:5

The seen curve of the wave is the physical cycle. It is the Day. The unseen curve is the after-death state. It is the Night. Both of these curves have various stages. It is easy to detect the stages of the seen cycle (Day). These are:

1. Birth/Infancy – First day
2. Childhood – Second day
3. Adolescence – Third day

4. Adulthood – Fourth day
5. Maturity – Fifth day
6. Death – Sixth day
7. Rest – Seventh day

Similarly, we can project that the stages of the unseen cycle (Night) are the following:

1. Birth into the spiritual state – First day
2. Period of adjustment – Second day
3. Review and evaluation of earthly experiences – Third day
4. Incorporation of lessons Learned – Fourth day
5. Decision to undergo one more cycle – Fifth day
6. Waiting for the opportune window of synchronicities – Sixth day
7. Birth into the physical realm with a clean slate and fresh start – Seventh day

The Seen Stages

We can easily relate to the seen stages because we have gone through them. We were born and experienced infancy, childhood, adolescence and adulthood. Some of us have made it to old age while many have passed away. Just as each cycle of birth has various stages, by the law of correspondence (As Above, So Below), cyclic immortality itself has its stages. Initially, most incarnations are at the infancy stage, learning and adjusting to physical life. We then go through the childhood stage, become adolescent, advance into adulthood and finally reach maturity. Each stage is like a "day" which might last hundreds or even thousands of years, requiring several incarnations.

This explains why people are so different. Each is in a different stage on the cyclic wave of immortality. Some are at the infancy and childhood stages. They are "new souls" at the mercy of their karma. These people are self-centered, childish and immature. They find themselves in untenable situations and complain frequently. Others are at the adolescent stage. They act foolishly and take unnecessary risks. Those who are adults, accept responsibility, complain less, do their best, learn and grow. Those who are mature are "old souls." They are sympathetic, compassionate and creative. They are content with their lives and are productive and wise.

People who question their status in life are oblivious to the role they play in attracting their circumstances. What they are now experiencing is often the result of previous actions or inaction. While we do not choose everything in our lives, we have a choice in how we act. We can resign ourselves to our "fate" and accept it as the will of God, or chance, or we can roll up our sleeves and take on our challenges as opportunities to learn from and improve. Through effort, determination and perseverance, we progress to a more desirable situation. We can alter our destiny by taking simple, small steps in the right direction. Every positive act makes a difference.

As we progress in our development, we become more aware of the consequences of our actions and we prevent "bad" Karma. Based on the level of our consciousness, we begin to exercise more freedom in where we end up on the ladder of life. Once fully awake, we can choose most of our circumstances.

The Unseen Stages

The first two stages in the unseen cycle are birth into the spiritual state and a period of adjustment. When people die, they enter unfamiliar territory. How we transition from physicality into the spiritual state varies from person to person. What we experience depends on circumstance and belief.

Some who are afraid to die, resist and hold on to dear life. These people require an incentive to let go and die. This can be a vision of relatives and familiar figures inviting them to move on. Pain, suffering and hopelessness also are an incentive to let go and die. Others see spiritual figures from their religions. Many who have had near-death experiences report seeing a tunnel of light and following it. These are aids to comfort and enable us to transition to our new state.

The remaining stages in the unseen cycle are similar for everyone. After adjusting to our new state, we get to review, evaluate and incorporate lessons learned from our earthly experiences. Once we decide that we want another go at life in a body, we wait for the perfect circumstances. Then we are born once more as babies with a brand-new set of opportunities.

◆ ◆ ◆

Cyclic immortality is a grand scheme. It is magic. It is as if it is Ground Hog Day over and over. Few things are as good as the first time. That is why we seek new and ever more challenging thrills. They afford us the opportunity to experience events for the first time.

With each rebirth, we can experience a brand-new embrace. Is there anything more exhilarating than our first embrace? With each rebirth we can enjoy our first kiss. Is there anything more enjoyable than our first kiss? We can fall in love again for the first time. Is there anything more exciting than our first love? We can be awed at the birth of our first child. Is there anything more thrilling than the experience of having our first child? Or even our first marriage, especially if it is to the right person.

Over eons of time, we can be great athletes, politicians, leaders, artists, scientists or any other profession we fancy or imagine. We can also choose to be ordinary, poor and even handicapped. Furthermore, with each new cycle, our options increase due to new discoveries and innovations. Cyclic immortality avails us unlimited options to choose from.

What if we could live in any country we liked, would we always live in the same area?

What if we could live anywhere we wanted? Would we always live in the same house even if it is a mansion?

What if we could marry any person we wanted, would we always pick the same individual?

If we could select between being poor or wealthy, would we always choose wealth?

If we were always wealthy, how would we know what it is like to be poor?

If we are always poor, how would we know what it is like to be wealthy?

If we had a choice, would we always choose to be healthy and strong? If we did, how would we know how the sick and the feeble feel?

With cyclic existence we can be both and every other state in between. We can have our cake and eat it, too. It is my greatest revelation and the supreme brainchild of the universe.

Cyclic existence is absolutely the most ingenious way for immortals to live. It binds the boundless, limits the limitless, and confers mortality to immortals. Cyclic existence ensures endless waves of newness, innovation, surprise, excitement and unlimited diverse ways to live and to experience.

The beauty of this revelation is its simplicity. It explains all the mysteries surrounding life and death. Since Occam's Razor states that, of all explanations that account for all the facts, the simpler one is more likely to be correct, I claim that cyclic immortality is the simplest explanation of the mysteries of life and is true.

I am thrilled that I had the experience of discovering cyclic immortality for myself. So, hail to living and experiencing. Halleluiah to cyclic immortality. It makes the barren productive, the ugly beautiful, and the meaningless worthwhile. Cyclic existence is by far the best innovation of being. With it, we can press the "reset" button and be renewed. Without it, entropy would triumph and living would revert to a nightmarish hell.

QUESTIONS TO CONSIDER

By doubting we are led to question, by questioning we arrive at the truth.   *– Peter Abelard*

1. Why Are We Genetically Programmed To Age And Die?

Since life has been evolving on planet Earth for over 2 billion years, all features selected are because they provide an existential advantage. Aging and death are no exceptions. They are selected and persist because they are beneficial. How can this be? Not all benefits are obvious. Aging and death serve our ultimate purpose to live forever via cyclic immortality. They make our exits possible. We have lived, aged and died numerous times. We age and die so we may be born again.

In my book, **<u>Listening to The Voice Within, becoming enlightened,</u>** I explain that death must have been the result of natural selection. Now, I understand why. The fundamental reason we let go and die, is the deep-seated, yet unconscious knowledge that we, in fact, do not die. We have done this many times before. We know that there is no real death, but a mere transition from one state to another. Death is always an invited guest, albeit begrudgingly, fearfully and instinctively. Death is never a usurper. In my book, **_A Passion for Living, a Path to Meaning and Joy_**, I give 8 reasons why we choose to die. I also describe, in detail, many of the contributors to aging and eventual death.

2. Why Not Choose The Best Life Possible, Every Time?

Most of what we experience is the result of our previous actions or inaction – karma. Only those spiritually awake can choose their circumstances. Regardless, if we could choose any type of life, would we always choose the best that life has to offer? What if we were all-powerful royalties and all of our wishes were always fulfilled? How much of life can we really enjoy? For how long? After a while, we will require ever increasing stimulation to be satisfied and eventually boredom will set in.

There is a vast difference in what we choose depending on whether we have one life to live or an infinite number of lives. In one lifetime, we might choose the best of circumstances believing that it would be the only time we would experience them. Over thousands of lifetimes, however, we would not make the same choices. We would crave new experiences, even painful ones.

It is a blessing that our lives are not perfect. If our lives were perfect and we had no lacks, would we still have desires, ambitions, or anything to look forward to? Would our lives still be worth living? It is the challenges of life that make living worthwhile. We chose to live this life in this particular way because of its trials and tribulations, its pleasures and exhilarations. Perfection is boring. Sameness is tedious. Having everything kills motivation. We choose diverse experiences because this is how we encounter new, exciting and adventurous opportunities. As a result, we grow.

Being eternal, we have all the time in the world to experience everything. Experiencing only success, pleasure and happiness does not lead to growth. It becomes monotonous, routine and boring after many repetitions. Imagine playing Solitaire and winning every time. Where is the fun in that? We crave diversity, challenge and even pain because we are eternal. We are not victims. Experiences are invited guests. Diverse, even challenging experiences sustain us.

3. Why Is Life So Short?

We are born with a purpose. Once our purpose is accomplished, we leave, unless we choose another. How long it takes to achieve our purpose varies. That is why each individual has a different life span, some shorter than others.

The fact that people have different life spans makes life mysterious. We do not know when we might die. Boredom is another reason we do not live extremely long lives. Boredom is an archenemy of humankind. Eventually, it will set in and suck the joy out of living. We might enjoy doing something a few times, but when we have eternity, it is an entirely different ball game. If we had very long lives in one body, it is only a matter of time before we run out of options. There is one and only one solution to boredom for immortals – cyclic existence. There is one and only one solution to life span for mortals –individual purpose. If our life purpose requires us to live long lives, then we do. Otherwise, we do not. Since we set our own purpose for each life, we determine how long each life will be.

The same way that each sport has a time limit, so it is with our lives. While sports have an agreed upon duration, our life span depends on our purpose which is seldom known. Thus, how long we will live in each lifetime remains a mystery. To live a meaningful life and to accomplish worthwhile achievements, our lives must be limited with an end date in sight. We are born with an expiration date. Not knowing when we might die makes living urgent. Not knowing if we have another day to live, we get to savor everything more intensely. Having short lives, we get to cherish our days. We get to accomplish far greater deeds in the short time allotted us.

How much more can we relish a lover's embrace, the perfume of a flower, a sunrise or sunset, the birth of a child, knowing that these are momentary experiences? They are here now and gone forever in a short while.

If we fully realize how short our lives are, we can live as if we were terminal patients with only a few months to live. We can make every moment count and every encounter precious. We do not know how many days we have to live. We should savor each one of them for we could die tomorrow. That is why Christ gave us the parable of the rich man.

And he told them a parable, saying, "The land of a rich man produced plentifully, and he

> *thought to himself, 'What shall I do, for I have nowhere to store my crops?' And he said, 'I will do this: I will tear down my barns and build larger ones, and there I will store all my grain and my goods. And I will say to my soul, "Soul, you have ample goods laid up for many years; relax, eat, drink, be merry."' But God said to him, 'Fool! This night your soul is required of you, and the things you have prepared, whose will they be?'*   Luke 12:16-20

We should plan for a long and healthy life. At the same time, we should live as if we could die tomorrow. Life is precious because it is short, temporary and unpredictable.

4. What If We Are Just As The Beasts Are, With Only One Life To Live?

If we are mere beasts and we have only one life to live, life would indeed be a tragic accident. What is the sense of learning, improving, planning and sacrificing if we are going to die and lose all? In this case, hedonism would make sense and the Biblical statement:

> *So I saw that there is nothing better than that a man should enjoy his work, for that is his lot; who can bring him to see what will be after him?*   Ecclesiastes 3:22

would be the only sensible way to live. Hence, the best way to use up our allotted time here on Earth would be to eat, drink, and be merry. We would focus on pleasure at the exclusion of all else. We would be selfish and take advantage of every opportunity to gratify ourselves. Yet, that is not how we live. Deep down, in our heart, we know that there is more to life than a one-time experience. We know that our lives matter. That is why we care. That is why there is philanthropy. That is why people willingly sacrifice for the welfare of others, even strangers. Our knowledge is not intellectual. It is ingrained in us as instinct. Often, we act based on "gut-feelings." Even though we cannot explain our actions, they give us comfort and the feeling that we are not misguided. We know that death is not the end-all. We know that we are immortal, yet we cannot explain it. We sacrifice ourselves gladly because we know it is not the only life we have. We will live again.

5. Is Everyone Equally Immortal?

Everyone is immortal, yet not everyone is equally aware of their immortality. As will be explained later, we have two aspects to our existence: physical and spiritual. The physical is our body with its "operating system" of passions, urges and survival instinct. It also includes the ego and the lower emotions of rage, anger, hate, jealousy, revenge and vindictiveness. The body' urges, directed by the hormones, are not easy to resist. Many succumb to them. When the body dies, all these die with the body. Yet what lives on is the spiritual. It should be our main focus.

Our spiritual aspect is our soul with its "operating system" of our higher emotions of love, compassion, sympathy, understanding, tolerance, forgiveness and empathy. These are aspects of our "epi-soul". They are our "spiritual capital". We add to our "spiritual capital" every time we engage our spiritual "operating system", and when we use our creativity, imagination, visualization, sense of wonder and gratitude.

The bigger our "spiritual capital", the more alive, conscious and aware we are of our "immortality". These are our "talents" that we must multiply. These are the treasures of heaven that do not spoil. We are born to manage our physical urges, transmute them and add to our immortality factor. As our "spiritual capital" grows, we become more aware of our special gifts such as extra-sensory perception and of our immortality. Ultimately, we will become conscious co-creators with divinity.

6. What If There Is No Cyclic Immortality?

Obviously, I could be wrong. However, the knowledge regarding cyclic immortality is not book-knowledge. I experienced it firsthand. Additionally, it is empowering, ennobling and liberating. It puts us at the helm of our lives. It makes us responsible for our beliefs. It allows us to live the consequences of our actions. It explains the mysteries and it does not diminish our self-worth. What are the alternatives? Dust to dust and total oblivion? A belief in judgement? An abode in heaven or hell? Victims of circumstance? Cyclic immortality is not only logical, it is visceral and intuitive. We do not have to accept this proposition as true if it does not make sense to us or resonate within us as true. We can, however, entertain the concept until we can validate it to our satisfaction. What do we have to lose? It is the most empowering of all alternatives. Why not go with it?

7. Why Don't We Remember Our Immortality?

We only remember what helps our current existence. Remembering our immortality does not. Hence, it is filtered out. Because we forget our immortality, we fear death and we appreciate the temporary nature of our existence.

Remembering our immortality is an impediment to fully enjoying life. If we did remember our immortality, most likely, we would neglect our bodies. We would live dangerously and with abandon knowing that we cannot die. We would be less careful regarding injury. We would take foolish risks. We would become lazy, unmotivated to accomplish and reach goals simply because we have eternity to do it. We might also miss out on experiencing important emotions such as fear, worry, concern, and agony. Our enjoyment of life would diminish drastically. Hence, it is best to forget that we are immortals.

We never completely forget anything. Our lives are a reflection of everything we have encountered so far. Therefore, just because we consciously do not remember something does not mean that we have forgotten it completely. Important memories become part of our character and personality. We are far more than what we are conscious of. We have a vast subconscious and are connected to a limitless superconscious.

Consciously, we only remember the main events of our lives, yet our subconscious stores all of our memories in the background. This includes the memory of our immortality. Over time, these subconscious memories become instincts and shape aspects of our character and personalities. Since the memory of our immortality is instinctive, we do not hesitate to sacrifice our lives. We know we will live again.

PART III

The Proof

WHAT CONSTITUTES PROOF?

For those who believe, no proof is necessary. For those who don't believe, no proof is possible.   −Stuart Chase

Proof Vs. Truth

Can we prove that cyclic immortality is true?

I cannot prove it for you, you have to do it for yourself. I will present you with evidence to consider. In the final analysis, your own mind, heart and experiences have to be your guide. Never-the-less, we cannot reject cyclic immortality just because it does not jive with our current beliefs.

What are our current beliefs? Have we examined them? What evidence is there to support them? Written accounts in books do not constitute evidence or proof. Matters of life and death cannot be dogma. We are intelligent beings. We have minds to think, hearts to feel and a guide within to know by. These can lead us to the truth.

Before we believe or disbelieve, accept or reject a proposal, we must have an open mind. We cannot be defending a "truth" we accepted from our childhood when we were impressionable. Our culture indoctrinates us with beliefs stemming from our religion. These are often accepted without study, analysis or a shred of evidence. We cannot reject something new just because of established beliefs.

I was born a Christian and grew up as one. I, too, had many unevaluated beliefs. Yet, when my experiences pointed me in a different direction, I did not object or resist. I kept an open mind. As the evidence mounted, I changed my views. I accepted cyclic immortality conditionally until something better presented itself. I would rather know than believe. I do not want to defend systems; I want to know the truth. I am still a Christian, but I have my own understanding as to what that means. My focus shifted from sin and salvation to ennobling love and empowering service.

I am not presenting a theory of reincarnation, something I know little about. What I am presenting is experiential evidence that supports cyclic immortality as a valid possibility. This discovery was a revelation. It came as an answer to my persistent questioning. You, however, do not have to accept it. Just entertain it and allow for your own evidence to accumulate and convince you because of your experiences and not because you read it here.

For some, no amount of evidence is enough. They are never convinced. That is their prerogative. Skepticism is natural, welcomed and healthy. However, there is a limit to skepticism and how much and how well we can prove anything. We can engage in endless debates and waste our precious time instead of enjoying the benefits of the revelation.

I witnessed this during the Covid epidemic. For

those who got vaccinated, the science behind the vaccine was sufficient. For the unvaccinated, however, no amount of evidence was enough, not even the number of people who died from Covid. People chose to believe without any evidence and accept obviously fabricated data to support their emotional and political convictions. Recently, a close relative told me of a Center for Disease Control (CDC) report that shows more vaccinated people are dying from Covid than unvaccinated people. Talk about fake news!

There is a simple way to compare two beliefs. Conduct a pro/con analysis. Compare your beliefs to the new proposal item by item. Look at the mysteries list (Part 4.) How do your current religious teachings explain the mysteries? Compare that to cyclic immortality. Which one makes more sense? Be honest. Go with what resonates with you. Be fearless. If one rings truer than the other, accept it conditionally until something better comes along.

My measure of truth is personal experience coupled with logic, reason, analysis and inner knowing. I also observe and study nature. If an answer resolves the issues in question and resonates as "true" and is empowering, then I accept the evidence as true until supplanted by a better account. True answers are usually simple, elegant, empowering, and liberating. The revelation I received regarding immortality passes this litmus test. It is based on personal experience, observation, and inner knowing, and it "fits" in the sense that it explains many of the mysteries surrounding us. It also has the added benefit of being reassuring and empowering. If we are immortal, what is there to worry about or fear? We can dive full force into the stream of life and celebrate our experiences regardless of their nature. Keeping in mind that no one knows the duration of any one cycle, we can fully appreciate our experiences while they last. The situations we find ourselves in, our current circumstances, will be gone shortly, never to return again. Not knowing when this cycle might end, it is best to appreciate and enjoy the people we know while we have them. When we meet them again, they will be under a different guise. We might not even recognize them.

Believability is not a criterion for truth. Life is full of facts that are hard to believe that are also true. Here is a short sample:

1. There are more living organisms on and inside of us than there are people on Earth. There are more bacteria in and on us than our own cells. We house 39 trillion bacteria compared to only 30 trillion of our own cells.
2. The population of insects is a billion times greater than the human population.
3. Human saliva contains a painkiller, Opiorphin, which is 10 times more powerful than morphine.
4. Stomach acid is strong enough to dissolve razor blades.
5. A dog can detect a teaspoon of sugar in a million gallons of water.
6. What we think of as solid matter is in fact empty space.
7. The reality we experience is the mere creation and projection of the mind. The brain receives

sensory data in the form of electrical impulses, translates these, then constructs and projects a world for us to experience.

If nature can produce incredibly sophisticated compounds such as DNA, RNA, enzymes, hormones, neurotransmitters, hemoglobin and chlorophyl, it can easily come up with an ingenious way to preserve life – cyclic immortality.

If nature, imbued with consciousness, can produce a brain as sophisticated as the human brain, it can definitely come up with cyclic immortality. Just imagine what the brain can do. From sensory data it creates a world for us to experience. We can see, hear, reason, imagine and be inspired. Just because we do not understand how these are done does not mean that they do not happen. The brain is the product of evolutionary forces directed by consciousness. Why can't these same forces allow for cyclic immortality to be a reality? Evolution has "selected" beneficial traits for living creatures. Why not select eternal life as well? If life can happen, why not eternal life? Why not cyclic immortality?

The riddle of mortality has indeed been solved and the solution is ingenious.

"O death, where is your victory? O death, where is your sting?" 1Cor 15:55

Through cyclic existence, death is vanquished and life is preserved with endless opportunities for renewal. We are at once eternal and temporal, immortal and mortal.

How wonderful!

How miraculous!

How ingenious!

How utterly godly!

THE EVIDENCE

What can be asserted without evidence can be dismissed without evidence. – Christopher Hitchens

Science deals with facts and proof while spirituality's domain is evidence and truth. While we cannot prove or disprove spiritual concepts, we can offer evidence in support of them. Truth is something we feel in our hearts. We know truth by its "fruit. It sets us free.

and you will know the truth, and the truth will set you free.   John 8:32

For now, let us accept cyclic immortality as a theory. Over time, a theory becomes law if and when it resolves all the issues that it is explaining in the simplest way (Occam's Razor). This revelation does just that. Give it time and it will become self-evident.

The evidence will be presented in two segments: first, we must demonstrate that soul is real since it is the soul that experiences cyclic immortality. Next, we will provide evidence that the soul does indeed undergo cyclic immortality.

◆ ◆ ◆

SOUL, FACT OR FICTION

A beautiful woman delights the eye; a wise woman, the understanding; a pure one, the soul.
— Minna Antrim

How can we know for sure that we have a soul? Should we accept that we have a soul because we have been told so? What if this is not true? How can we find out for ourselves?

We are told many "truths". We hear a lot about the soul from our religions, philosophers, parents and peers. Many accept that we must have souls because it is written in "holy" books, taught by prophets, or inspired people. What if they are wrong? Statements in books and the teachings of others should be information until we have experiences that validate that information. Then, it becomes experienced knowledge. Ultimately, the only proof that counts is that which we can demonstrate ourselves. We must be convinced because of **our** experiences, logic, and inner knowing. **It is easy to believe. It is far more difficult to validate and know for sure.** It takes effort, intention and persistence to arrive at satisfying answers. When I desperately wanted to know if I had a soul, I was blessed by a near-death experience. From it, I **knew** that my soul was my identity. I **AM** my soul.

What follows is not an exhaustive exposition of the validity of the soul. These are a few insights to share and guide us to sources that are wellsprings of experiential understanding. I have lived and experienced several of these. I urge you to evaluate your own experiences and see how much evidence you can come up with that will satisfy you. Do not take anyone else's word for it. If something is important, validate it to your own satisfaction before you reject it as false or accept it as true. At a minimum, keep an open mind.

WHAT IS SOUL?

The most powerful weapon on earth is the human soul on fire. — Ferdinand Foch

What exactly is soul?

When I had my near-death experience, one fact stood out – I had two types of animating factors: **spirit** and **soul**. Spirit is the "operating system" of the body. It is the same for all living creatures. Soul, on the other hand, is the "specialized software", unique to each individual.

Every living creature is endowed with spirit. This is what makes us as the beasts are. With spirit, we have only the functions necessary for survival such as awareness of self and surroundings, eating, drinking, sleeping, digesting, breathing, walking, mating and communicating. With spirit we strive to survive, compete, get angry, experience fear and the rest of the lower emotions. If we only follow our urges and are controlled by our hormones, we are "Earth Bound." With only a spirit, we have no advantage over the beasts as Ecclesiastes states. We have none of the higher functions. We follow our instincts. We cannot think of a past or a future. We are always in the now concerned with ourselves and survival. Spirit houses the ego, the urges, and the passions. Spirit is our lower self. When the body dies, so does the spirit.

Soul is our immortal essence. It has two parts: a core which I call **basic soul** and a periphery which I term **epi-soul**. Just as an atom has a core of protons and neutrons and a periphery of orbiting electrons, our soul consists of a "central" basic soul and an "expanded" epi-soul.

Basic soul is our original gift from God. It is the one "talent" we started life with. It is our core identity and it never changes. We are expected to invest this one talent and add to it by living wisely, learning from our experiences, growing and maturing. As we do, we build our epi-soul around our basic soul. We augment our epi-soul via experiences and lessons learned. As our epi-soul grows, so do our individualized higher functions that distinguish us from beasts. Epi-soul enables us to view the past, project into the future, plan, reason, analyze, visualize, imagine, be creative, be intuitive and be inspired. With the growth of our epi-soul, our higher emotions of love, sympathy, empathy and compassion expand forming a "field" around the core – the basic soul. This field is our "spiritual capital." As our epi-soul grows, we begin to appreciate the sublime and experience extra-sensory perceptions. The "fruit" of the epi-soul are the treasures that do not spoil that Christ alluded to.

> *"Do not lay up for yourselves treasures on earth, where moth and rust destroy and where thieves break in and steal, but lay up for yourselves treasures in heaven, where neither moth nor rust destroys and where thieves do not break in and steal. For where your treasure is, there your heart will be also.* Matt 6:19-21

Spirit gives us life and awareness. Soul endows us with mind and consciousness. While spirit evolves naturally, soul must be developed individually by personal intent and effort. This is where freedom of choice and individual effort come into play. We determine how fast and how well our epi-souls develop and mature. Each individual is on their own path, advancing at their own pace. This is why every individual is different. Criminals who have no regard for others have embryonic epi-souls. By rising above our "bestiality", we add to our "spiritual capital" and our epi-soul grows and matures. As it does, we graduate from being simple (like hydrogen) to more advanced individuals (such as gold.) Once our epi-soul is developed enough, we retain the memories from previous incarnations and can mine our storehouse of knowledge gained from all of our past lives. Our realization of our immortality rests in our epi-soul since that determines the level of our consciousness. Once our consciousness is "high enough", we become conscious co-creators with God.

Soul is our true identity. It is who we are. It is our essence. We **have** a body, spirit, and emotions. What we **are**, however, is soul. We live in our bodies for as long as our soul remains attached to it via a "spiritual umbilical cord." When this cord detaches or is severed either through an accident or naturally, we die in the body, yet continue to live as soul.

◆ ◆ ◆

Evidence in Support of Soul

1. Out-Of-Body Experience

One of the best ways to prove the existence of the soul is to witness it out of the body. If we have an out-of-body experience (OBE), then we know for sure that we not only have a soul but that **we are** our soul. An OBE is not a theory. It is not a belief. It is **knowing**. I have had several of these beginning at an early age. Many people have had these experiences and there are several books that describe them in detail. Some books even teach how to have these experiences ourselves. Once we experience ourselves out of the body, our doubts will vanish just as darkness is dispelled when light shines.

2. Near-Death Experience

A near-death experience (NDE) is the ultimate OBE. Those who have had an NDE know the absolute reality of their souls. They have no fear of death because they know that they do not really die for they are eternal souls. Even if we have not had an NDE, we can talk to someone, or read the account of someone, who has had an NDE and learn from their experience. I too have had an NDE. This experience changed my life. I describe my NDE in detail in my book, **_A Passion for Living, a path to meaning and joy_**.

NDEs are more common than we realize. Many have experienced them and describe their accounts, especially some patients while undergoing surgery. Critically injured people have, on many occasions, left their bodies and returned later to describe their experiences. People who have had an NDE have a new perspective on life realizing that they have a mission to carry out. I had my NDE as an answer to my persistent questioning about whether or not I had a soul.

An NDE is a life altering experience. Once we have it, we have a keen knowing of what life is all about. We know that we are immortal. We know that death is a mere transition – a doorway to the other side where we reside before we are born and where we return after we pass away. With an NDE, we return to the same body. After death, we return to a new body as a baby.

3. Soul Visitations

Wouldn't it be great if a departed soul visited us personally? Wouldn't that be proof enough that the soul does indeed persist? I had such an experience. My mother visited me after she died while I was in a monastery. Her visit reassured me of the validity of the soul and its continued existence after death.

Many find comfort in the visitation of departed loved ones while asleep and dreaming. Additionally, many have experienced ghosts, hauntings, and apparitions. This is not to say that all these accounts are true and accurate. At the same time, we cannot dismiss them all as hoaxes. We can use our judgement as to what makes sense and what does not. There are kernels of truth scattered about and it is our job to discover them.

4. Biblical References

Spirits

> Do not turn to the spirits of the dead and do not seek familiar spirits to become unclean by them. I am the LORD your God.   Lev 19:31

> Now the Spirit of the LORD had turned away from Saul, and an evil spirit from the LORD tormented him.   1Sam 16:14

> Micaiah said, "That being the case, listen to the LORD's message. I saw the LORD sitting on his throne, with all the heavenly assembly standing beside him on his right and on his left. The LORD said, 'Who will deceive Ahab, so he will attack Ramoth Gilead and die there?' One said this and another that. Then a spirit stepped forward and stood before the LORD. He said, 'I will deceive him.' The LORD asked him, 'How?' He replied, 'I will go out and be a lying spirit in the mouths of all his prophets.' The LORD said, 'Deceive and overpower him. Go out and do as you have proposed.'   1 Kings 22:19-22

Calling Forth A Departed Soul

> So Saul inquired of the LORD, but the LORD did not answer him – not by dreams nor by Urim nor by the prophets. So Saul instructed his servants, "Find me a woman who is a medium, so that I may go to her and inquire of her." His servants replied to him, "There is a woman who is a medium in En Dor."
> So Saul disguised himself and put on other clothing and left, accompanied by two of his men. They came to the woman at night and said, "Use your ritual pit to conjure up for me the one I tell you."
> But the woman said to him, "Look, you are aware of what Saul has done; he has removed the mediums and magicians from the land! Why are you trapping me so you can put me to death?" But Saul swore an oath to her by the LORD, "As surely as the LORD lives, you will not incur guilt in this matter!" The woman replied, "Who is it that I should bring up for you?" He said, "Bring up for me Samuel."
> When the woman saw Samuel, she cried out loudly. The woman said to Saul, "Why have you deceived me? You are Saul!" The king said to her, "Don't be afraid! What have you seen?" The woman replied to Saul, "I have seen a divine spirit coming up from the ground!" He said to her, "What about his appearance?" She said, "An old man is coming up! He is wrapped in a

robe!"

Then Saul realized it was Samuel, and he bowed his face toward the ground and kneeled down. Samuel said to Saul, "Why have you disturbed me by bringing me up?" Saul replied, "I am terribly troubled! The Philistines are fighting against me and God has turned away from me. He does not answer me anymore – not by the prophets nor by dreams. So I have called on you to tell me what I should do."

Samuel said, "Why are you asking me, now that the LORD has turned away from you and has become your enemy? The LORD has done exactly as I prophesied! The LORD has torn the kingdom from your hand and has given it to your neighbor David! Since you did not obey the LORD and did not carry out his fierce anger against the Amalekites, the LORD has done this thing to you today. The LORD will hand you and Israel over to the Philistines! Tomorrow both you and your sons will be with me. The LORD will also hand the army of Israel over to the Philistines!"

1 Sam 28:6-21

5. Answer To Prayer

Have any of your prayers ever been answered in an unequivocal way? Did you ever pray for something in particular and knew right away that your request had been granted? I have. I asked to be guided to my soul mate, life partner, and future spouse. I was. If we can be certain that our prayers are heard, then we can be certain that we are watched over and cared for.

Who watches over us?

Who answers our prayers?

Many would say that Angels watch over us and that God answers our prayers. It is true. However, we can be more specific. I believe it is our Higher Self that always watches over us and answers our prayers. Our Higher Self is intimately connected to us and is inseparable from God. It is our personal angel, always aware of what is best for us. It is the one who inspires and guides us anytime we ask, seek and knock.

To get our prayers answered, we must first connect to our Higher Self via our higher faculties and noble emotions. We can use our imagination, visualization, love, and compassion to climb "Jacob's Ladder" and connect to our Higher Self. Once we do, we can ask, seek and knock. No selfish requests will ever be granted. No evil intentions will be heard. We cannot ask victory for ourselves at the expense of others. It does not work that way. In the higher realms, everyone, without exception is a child of God, dearly loved and equally appreciated.

6. Identity

Even though our bodies have been changing since conception, and our emotions and mental states have been maturing, there is a permanent aspect to our being. We always know who we are. There is continuity to ourselves. Our individuality, uniqueness, and identity are never in doubt. Even though our cells die and new ones are formed and even though the atoms composing our bodies are completely replaced every few years, we always know who we are regardless of any changes that we go through. This is because our basic soul remains changeless, ageless and inviolate. It never changes. It is the permanent aspect of our identity. Our epi-soul, on the other hand, changes. It grows. This allows us to change and remain changeless at the same time. We have a permanent identity that transcends any physical change we go through, yet we can continue to grow and mature. Our soul is our identity. Just as a seed is in the image of the plant it comes from; our soul is in the image of its source – God. Since God is immaterial, so are we as souls.

7. Inspiration And Extra-Sensory Perception

Have you ever been inspired, had a strong hunch, or a gut feeling about something and you were right? Where did the inspiration come from? Where did this gut feeling originate? These did not come from our brains because the information is brand new. These came to us but not from us, at least not the normal us. Where did they come from? They came from our Higher Self, the soul. If we learn to listen and act on our intuition, we will not only live healthier, happier and more prosperous and productive lives, we will get to know our innate reality as well. Our Higher Self communicates with us not only through **intuition and inspiration**, but also in our **dreams**, as our **conscience**, and as **The Voice Within**.

Extra-Sensory Perception (ESP) covers a range of

other functions: **Telepathy** (mind reading), is not easily demonstrable under lab conditions, but in everyday living, it happens routinely. It is especially evident between people who are close such as lovers, married couples and family members. I have experienced it numerous times. **Clairaudience** (perceiving what is inaudible from a distance), **Clairvoyance** (perceiving from a distance things or events in the present or the future), **Clairsentience** (perceiving or feeling things beyond normal sensory contact), and **Psychokinesis** (moving objects without physical contact). Perhaps ESP is a harbinger of abilities yet to manifest as we progress in our evolution. These are the gifts of our evolved epi-souls.

Have you ever wondered what the Holy Spirit was that descended on the Apostles during Pentecost? Or the dove that descended on Jesus during His baptism? Perhaps these were specialized packets of consciousness (epi-soul) with the advanced capabilities of ESP, healing power and the ability to communicate with people in their native tongue. Jesus might have had the extra capability to perform miracles. Perhaps these are the fruits of our future evolved epi-souls.

8. A Test

Have you ever told yourself that you wanted to wake up at a certain time and sure enough you wake up at exactly the time you specified? There are people with this ability. How is this possible? If this is a function of the brain, how can the brain tell conventional time? I know the body has a biological clock, but this is not the same as the ordinary clock that we have on the wall. We must have something that is beyond the body that complies with our intentions. There must be an aspect to us that is awake while we sleep. This aspect cannot be bound by the body, for conventional time is not in the body. We created conventional time to measure duration. What is this aspect that can wake us up at the exact time we specify? I attribute this aspect to our evolved epi-souls.

9. Coincidence/Synchronicity

The Oxford Languages Dictionary defines synchronicity as the simultaneous occurrence of events which appear significantly related but have no discernible causal connection. It also defines coincidence as a remarkable concurrence of events or circumstances without apparent causal connection. An occasional synchronicity could be a coincidence. When there are too many of them, there has to be a better explanation. There is. They are orchestrated by our Higher Selves, the soul.

I have talked to people who have had incredible synchronicities. My life is what it is because of synchronicities. There are too many to be coincidences. Here are a few:

- Had my mother not died, I would have never left Syria for Lebanon. Perhaps, I would have been killed in one of Syria's wars.
- Had I not run into Jean Holladay at the exact moment that I did, I would never have gone to college.

- Had I not failed my Biochemistry lab exam, I would have graduated sooner. I would have had to look for a job, a place to live and perhaps would have never immigrated to the United States. The reason I failed the exam was because the exam date was changed without my knowledge.
- If I had not failed my weapon's assembly test during my basic training at Ft. Dix, NJ., I would have never gone to Ft. Meade, MD. I would have graduated with a promotion, and gone to Fort Sam Houston in Texas.
- If I had not been discriminated against and bypassed for promotions repeatedly while working for a branch of the US Government, I would not have retired early, started my most rewarding career as a teacher and would not have written my recent books.
- Once we were locked out of our house because we left the house key inside. I suggested to my wife that we should go have a pizza and figure out what to do. While having the pizza, my brother and his wife, who lived far away, stopped by the same pizza place. Miraculously, he had our house keys in his car. He was the only one with an extra set of keys to our house.
- Had I not "accidentally" flipped through a magazine, seen and responded to an ad by the Rosicrucian Order, I would have never met and married my wife.
- If my uncle had not asked me to read that passage from Ecclesiastes, this book would not have been written.

- If we had not gone on the world cruise, my other book, **Listening to the Voice Within**, would not have been written.

The synchronicities in my life are not only numerous, but they shaped who I am. I do not believe these were due to chance. I firmly believe that our Higher Self, in conjunction with other people's Higher Selves, coordinate the critical events of our lives. Even though the major events of our lives are pre-planned, we can alter our course at any moment through the exercise of freedom of choice.

10. Religion

The existence of the soul is the most fundamental aspect of religion. It is assumed to be a gift from God. Yet, hardly any religion can explain exactly what soul is. How many souls are there? Were they created at the beginning of time? Do they appear at birth? Perhaps at conception?

There are many explanations of what the soul experiences after death. Yet, hardly any reference as to where souls were before birth. For religion, souls are eternal. However, anything that is eternal is timeless. It is eternal both before birth and after death. Souls must be eternal before we are born to be eternal after we die. There is no "starting point" for eternals.

CYCLIC IMMORTALITY, FACT OR FICTION

The great tragedy of science - the slaying of a beautiful hypothesis by an ugly fact. −Thomas Huxley

I prefer the term "cyclic immortality" rather than reincarnation because various groups have different understandings of what reincarnation is. Reincarnation, for me, is simply being born again in a physical body. Cyclic immortality is how the soul expresses its immortality.

Reincarnation, the idea of being born in a new body, is an ancient belief. According to Wikipedia, "The **idea of reincarnation** has roots in the Upanishads of the late Vedic period (c. 1100 – c. 500 BCE), predating the Buddha and the Mahavira. The concepts of the cycle of birth and death, samsara, and liberation partly derive from ascetic traditions that arose in India around the middle of the 1st millennium BCE."

The Encyclopedia Britannica states that "Plato, in the 5th–4th century BCE, believed in an immortal soul that participates in frequent incarnations." The ancient Egyptians mummified their dead because they believed that the spirit of the deceased will return to occupy the body. There are also groups of Jews, Christians and Muslims who believe in reincarnation. In fact, the vast majority of the people on planet Earth believe in reincarnation. Where did this belief come from? The human mind is capable of creating beliefs to fill voids, or as an answer to perplexing mysteries. Beliefs do not constitute evidence. There are too many interpretations of what reincarnation is and how it works. While living, we cannot know for sure the intricacies of reincarnation. We can, however, rely on our experiences and the personal experiences of reliable witnesses to glean precious insights. What I am promoting is not a belief in reincarnation as a system, rather I am advocating the immortality of the soul which relies on a form of reincarnation as the vehicle for cyclic immortality.

Evidence in Support of Cyclic Immortality

1. Quandary

I have traits and abilities that I do not know how or when I acquired them. I am one of six children born to parents who for all practical purposes were illiterate. We grew up destitute in a very oppressive environment. We spoke Armenian at home with our parents and also in school with friends. My parents spoke Turkish amongst themselves and with relatives. The language of the country was Arabic. My command of Arabic was shaky at best. That is until I went to high school in Sidon, Lebanon.

After leaving the monastery in Zahle, Lebanon, in February 1964, I attended high school in Sidon at the Gerard Institute. I had to wait until after Easter to start school. Since I came from a monastery and the school had been in session for several months, they did not know where to place me. I was given exams to determine my placement. My English was extremely poor. When I was asked to write an essay in Arabic, however, I had an astonishing discovery. I wrote the essay in about 15 minutes and handed it to the teacher, Mr. Dabaghy. The teacher read it, looked at me with a shocked expression and said nothing. He took the essay directly to the head of the Arabic Department, Mr. Youssif Abi Rizk.

Mr. Rizk returned to my class and read my essay to all the students. He then went on to read it to the other students in higher grades. This happened on numerous occasions whenever I wrote a new essay.

The next year, I had an unnerving incident. We had a new Arabic teacher, Mr. Baghdadi from Damascus, Syria. I wrote an essay in class and handed it over to him. In a few days, he returned the graded essays to us. My grade was "C." I was perplexed and shocked. I was shaking with frustration. I raised my hand and asked him:

Why did you give me a "C" for my essay?

"C" is a good grade for an Armenian, he said. You should be happy.

I am not happy. By the way, did you read the essay?, I asked.

I did not need to, he replied. I know that Armenians are poor at Arabic.

In that case, I refuse to be in your class, I said as I walked out.

I went to see Mr. Rizk and told him what happened. He called the teacher to his office and ordered him to read my essay and re-grade it. He did and he gave me an "A".

Where did my written mastery of Arabic come from? I had an imaginative style of writing that was reminiscent of a well-known Lebanese writer. How did this come about?

◆ ◆ ◆

In high school, I discovered that I had a passion for philosophy. I studied most of the ancient Greek philosophers. I also had a particular interest in Friedrich Nietzsche. I remember reading his book, **Thus Spoke Zarathustra** and having long discussions about it with my best friend Elias. Where did my love for philosophy come from?

I had another peculiarity that perplexed me. I was infatuated by Germany and German. In high school and college, I studied German, not French, like most Lebanese did. During the World Cup soccer tournaments, I would be the only one rooting for Germany. I never understood why. Years later, when I visited Germany, I felt at home. Why?

Later on in life, I had an irresistible urge to write and publish books. I majored in biology and worked in medicine and information systems. Where did my desire to write books come from? I have a highly developed imagination, and I am extremely confident and fearless in expressing my values. Where did these come from?

As a child, I knew that I was different. I wanted to know and understand why. I kept questioning myself. I persisted and began praying and meditating. One day while in meditative prayer, I had the answers I was seeking. Suddenly, completely, and out of the blue, it became clear to me. It all made sense. I was a German philosopher in my last life. I knew who I used to be and it explained my unusual interest with German, Germany and philosophy.

I did not know anything about reincarnation then. I was brought up a Christian. I studied in a monastery and was preparing to be a monk. Yet, when the revelation came, none of what I believed mattered. It made sense. I was satisfied and at peace.

I am not the only one attracted to a specific country or who has hidden talents and abilities. There are many. An interesting case is that of Dorothy Louise Eady, who knew she used to be a priestess in Ancient Egypt from a young age. Here is a very brief account of her life: (Please search her online and read her fascinating story. You will be amazed.)

> *Dorothy Louise Eady, also known as Omm Sety or Om Seti (16 January 1904 – 21 April 1981) was a British antiques caretaker and folklorist. She was keeper of the Abydos Temple of Seti I and draughtswoman for the Department of Egyptian Antiquities. She is especially well known for her belief*

that in a previous life she had been a priestess in ancient Egypt, as well as her considerable historical research at Abydos. Her life and work has been the subject of many articles, television documentaries, and biographies. (Wikipedia)

2. Child Prodegies

During the evening news on Friday, May 28, 2021, there was mention of a 2-year-old who was inducted into Mensa, the High IQ Society. Here is that report:

> Kashe Quest has become the youngest American member of Mensa at only 2 years old, KABC reported. Kashe has an IQ of 146, or about 50 points higher than average Americans. She not only can count to 100, read full sentences and identify all 50 states, she also has memorized the periodic table, KABC reported.

The 2021 season of America's Got Talent (AGT) featured 9-year-old opera singer, Victory Brinker. She made AGT history when she received the Golden Buzzer from all 5 collectively, 4 judges and the host. She stunned the judges and the audience with her performance. She became the first ever to receive the Golden Buzzer from all 5.

On the Thursday evening CBS news with Norah O'Donnell, Jamie Yuccas shared the story of a young boy (6 years-old) "who has become a pint-sized prodigy. He already knows the capitals of every state and country in the world—and he hasn't even reached kindergarten."

History is full of child prodigies. Among them: Wolfgang Amadeus Mozart, John von Neumann, Sor Juana Inés de la Cruz, Srinivasa Ramanujan, Stevie Wonder, and Blaise Pascal. Who are these prodigies and where does their talent come from? Cyclic immortality easily explains this mystery. Just as I could "remember" and tap some of my skills developed in a previous life, these prodigies tap into their previously mastered skills. Since we have had numerous incarnations, anyone can tap into skills previously developed. This is called "mining the Akash."

3. Mystery Of Character And Personality

No two individuals are identical. Yet, we are composed of the same few elements. What distinguishes us from each other are the intangibles: experiences and memory; talents, skills and abilities; character and personality.

Character and personality are essential aspects of a person. Yet each of us has a unique character and an inviolate personality. Where do our unique and distinguishing qualities come from? Since each member in the same family has a different personality, it is difficult to attribute these to genetics and environment alone. Parents with 2 or more children know how different each child can be. Even identical twins have character differences. Yet, we do not know why. We do know, however, that each child, at an early age, displays his or her unique qualities.

We are not born Tabula Rasa. Our subconscious memories are not limited to conception, gestation and birth. We come with a storehouse of latent memories, skills and abilities. We carry the memories of lessons learned from previous lives. I believe each new generation is more mature than the previous one because of these memories.

Trauma leaves an indelible mark on our subconscious. Imagine drowning in a past life. Fear of water, oceans and swimming might persist. Imagine being stabbed to death or being beheaded in a past life. Fear of sharp objects might endure. Imagine being struck by lightning and dying as a child in a past life. Extreme caution and aversion to having children might linger in the subconscious. Residues of past lives are always within us. Many are born with, not only fears and phobias, but also special talents, skills and preferences. These are past life memories.

4. Mystery Of Relationships

Who do we fall in love with? Who are our spouses and why did we get attracted to them? Who are our children, siblings, friends and people we feel close to? They are the ones we subconsciously recognize, remember and have agreed to be related to because of previous life associations.

When our youngest daughter was about 3-years old, she told me who she was in her prior life. Much later, our first born told me who she thought she was in her previous life. There are thousands of people, especially in the far east, who remember their previous lives in great detail. These cases are well documented in several books on the topic of reincarnation.

The people in our lives are exactly the ones we need in order to face our shortcomings, be challenged, and learn from. They are also the ones with whom we share our time, memories, heartaches and joys. Love and deep abiding friendships carry across lifetimes. Lovers, family members and friends tend to stick together through lifetimes. Enemies incarnate together to face each other and resolve conflicts.

We are exactly where we need to be. We are in the country of our choice, surrounded by people we have known. Our environment is exactly what we need to overcome challenges, celebrate victories and to renew and enjoy the company of friends and loved ones.

5. Mystery Of Preferences

Is where we choose to live accidental? Are the foods we prefer to consume random? Are the countries we enjoy visiting haphazard? Is the manner of our lives due to chance? I do not think so.

I lived my first five months in the United States in Massachusetts. It was only when I moved to Maryland that I felt at home. I have been living in Maryland since October 1972. I had several opportunities to move away, but resisted. Why?

I also have a favorite animal, the Buffalo, or the American bison. Seeing a Buffalo is always an emotional experience. Why? Is this a whimsical choice and an irrelevant emotion? I do not believe so, since later I remembered one of my past lives as a Native American.

Why do I spend hours listening to Edith Piaf when I hardly understand a word she is singing? One night in a dream I had the revelation that, in a previous life, I had been a one-legged French pirate. Our preferences are often due to buried memories that we are seldom aware of. They reveal to us who we have been. They are our history.

6. No True Beginning, Just Cycles

The cyclic nature of existence is evident everywhere. Every 7-days we start a new week. Every 30 days or so, we start a new month. Every 12-months, we start a new year. We have summer, fall, winter and spring and then the cycle starts all over. We are born, grow, mature, age and die. Does this cycle repeat itself as well?

Some cycles are short and we can easily detect them. Others are much longer. A few are so long that they escape our detection. Even though we cannot be aware of all cycles, there is a witness to cyclic existence. It is our soul. Our soul remembers all of our past lives. We do not know when the first cycle of cyclic immortality began. We do know, though, that the cycles of birth, death and rebirth will go on indefinitely.

The Bhagavad Gita states: *"Never was there a time when I did not exist, nor you, nor all these kings; nor in the future shall any of us cease to be. As the embodied soul continuously passes, in this body, from childhood to youth to old age, the soul similarly passes into another body at death. A sober person is not bewildered by such a change;"*

and *"Worn-out garments are shed by the body; Worn-out bodies are shed by the dweller within the body. New bodies are donned by the dweller, like garments." (Blogs.siliconindia.com)*

We never had a beginning as spiritual entities. We will never experience an end. Conception, birth and death are mere milestones. As souls, we are eternal. We undergo cyclic existence voluntarily. It is a preferable way to spend eternity. Facing challenges, enjoying acquaintances, learning, and creating a world of our choosing is the best way to pass our time. What else can we do when we have eternity to deal with?

7. Sleep

It is a mystery as to why we sleep. The heart does not sleep, neither does the brain, or any of our systems such as the circulatory. The body as a whole, however, must sleep. Why?

Sleep puts us in a vulnerable state. It poses a danger to our wellbeing. We are helpless while asleep. Each sleep is like a mini-death. We cannot resist sleep.

Is it possible that we sleep because, by the law of correspondence (As Above, So Below), the nature of our lives is cyclic? Just as we cycle through sleep and wakefulness, we cycle through life and death. While we wake up from sleep refreshed, we wake up from death fresh in a new body.

8. Law Of Conservation

Science teaches the law of conservation of energy and matter. I believe there is a similar law of conservation of consciousness. Our essence – soul – is conscious energy. It was not born and it can never be destroyed. Upon death, it merely leaves the body and enters a new state.

9. Occam's Razor

Cyclic immortality is the simplest explanation for all the mysteries. By definition, the simplest explanation is usually the most accurate, I propose that cyclic immortality is true and makes complete sense.

10. Biological Cyclic Immortality

We share the same DNA with all life forms – from the mosquito to elephants, to snakes and bats. This is because the same life force that began on planet Earth courses through us all. Whether life originated on Earth or hitched a ride from outer space, it is still that original DNA that reproduced itself through the evolutionary line until it reached us. Life persists on earth through cyclic existence.

Examining the human line of evolution beginning with our earliest ancestors and ending with us we find two types of cells that follow two different paths in how they reproduce. One cell line is the somatic and the other is the reproductive. Somatic cells are the cells of the body which include nerve cells, skin cells, and blood cells. Somatic cells divide via mitosis where one cell becomes two each with two sets of chromosomes in their nucleus – one from each parent. Somatic cells live while the body lives and die with the demise of the body and that is the end of their line.

Reproductive cells, on the other hand, are the eggs and sperms also known as germ cells or gametes. They divide via meiosis where each new cell has a single set of chromosomes. While somatic cells have a finite ability to reproduce and eventually die, reproductive cells continue their line indefinitely. They spread throughout humanity like wild fire. While most of the eggs of a female and the vast majority of the sperms of a male die, a few continue their journey via fertilization, gestation, and finally birth as new babies. Babies grow producing their line of eggs and sperms which continue the progression of life. Thus, the original germ cells continue living on indefinitely through future children and their descendants. This is how life has been perpetuating itself – cyclic immortality via the reproductive cells. We received our reproductive cells from our parents. They in turn received theirs from their parents going back to the beginning of life. Our children receive their reproductive cells from us and pass them to their children, thus ensuring that the line of the original reproductive cells continues indefinitely. In other words, this is biological cyclic immortality. If this is possible for germ cells, could it also be the process by which we, as souls, continue our existence indefinitely through cyclic immortality?

Why Do Cells Divide?

One of the greatest miracles we can witness is the birth of a child. This would never happen if the cell did not "know" how to divide. Why do cells divide is a question I once asked my professor at the American University of Beirut. His answer? We do not ask why questions in science, only how questions.

I have come to believe that a cell divides because it is imbued with consciousness. Consciousness is the director, the architect and the intelligence behind life.

There are two types of cell divisions:

1. Somatic cells divide to ensure the survival of the individual. This is the source of our powerful instinct to survive.
2. Sex cells (eggs and sperms) divide to ensure the survival of the species. This is the source of our powerful instinct to mate and reproduce.

When individuals survive, they can have earthly experiences. When the species survives, diversification becomes possible. With diversification, the option to form mastermind groups becomes available. With the formation of mastermind groups, life can evolve, advance and new features continue to be "created" and introduced.

With the birth of each child, newness is introduced into the world. With newness, experiences can continue, boredom is vanquished and eternal beings have a playground for endless varieties of experiences.

Biblical References

11. Old Testament

There is a tantalizing reference to cyclic immortality in the Old Testament, **an incredible reference to Lucifer reborn as king of Tyre**: (A city in Southern Lebanon)

A Lament over the King of Tyre (Ezekiel 28:11-19)

> Moreover, the word of the LORD came to me: "Son of man, raise a lamentation over the king of Tyre, and say to him, Thus says the Lord GOD:
> "You were the signet of perfection, full of wisdom and perfect in beauty.
> You were in Eden, the garden of God; every precious stone was your covering, sardius, topaz, and diamond, beryl, onyx, and jasper, sapphire, emerald, and carbuncle; and crafted in gold were your settings and your engravings.
> On the day that you were created they were prepared.
> You were an anointed guardian cherub. I placed you; you were on the holy mountain of God; in the midst of the stones of fire you walked.
> You were blameless in your ways from the day you were created, till unrighteousness was found in you.
> In the abundance of your trade you were filled with violence in your midst, and you sinned; so I cast you as a profane thing from the mountain of God, and

I destroyed you, O guardian cherub, from the midst of the stones of fire. Your heart was proud because of your beauty; you corrupted your wisdom for the sake of your splendor. I cast you to the ground; I exposed you before kings, to feast their eyes on you. By the multitude of your iniquities, in the unrighteousness of your trade you profaned your sanctuaries; so I brought fire out from your midst; it consumed you, and I turned you to ashes on the earth in the sight of all who saw you. All who know you among the peoples are appalled at you; you have come to a dreadful end and shall be no more forever."

Imagine that – Lucifer ruling on Earth as king of Tyre.

12. New Testament

There are also a couple of puzzling verses in the New Testament that allude to cyclic immortality:

1. Some believed that Jesus was John the Baptist reborn.

At that time Herod the tetrarch heard reports about Jesus, and he said to his servants, "This is John the Baptist. He has been raised from the dead! And because of this, miraculous powers are at work in him." Matt 14:1-2

2. Others believed that Jesus was Elijah, Jeremiah or one of the prophets.

When Jesus came to the area of Caesarea Philippi, he asked his disciples, "Who do people say that the Son of Man is?" They answered, "Some say John the Baptist, others Elijah, and others Jeremiah or one of the prophets." Matt16:13-14

PART IV

The Mysteries

THE MYSTERIES

> *Life and consciousness are the two great mysteries. Actually, their substrates are the inanimate. And how do you get from neurons shooting around in the brain to the thought that pops up in your head and mine? There's something deeply mysterious about that. And if you're not struck by the mystery, I think you haven't thought about it.*
>
> – Charles Krauthammer

"Touching Heaven" is the epitome of human emotions. It is a marriage made in heaven. It happens when the "fit" is absolute – the fit between the question and the answer, the male and the female, the mystery and the solution, the human and the divine.

Many live based on beliefs inherited from parents, society and culture. If these beliefs empower, enlighten and liberate, then they are "good" beliefs. Unfortunately, many of our beliefs are meant to instill fear in us so we obey and follow. Some of our beliefs even diminish our dignity by having us believe that we are not worthy of the best that life has to offer. These beliefs take away our self-esteem by instilling the guilt of "sin" in our hearts. When I was young and impressionable, I was taught that, on my own, I can never achieve "salvation." In fact, I was so bad that I required a blood sacrifice – that of the Son of God. Knowing that I had done nothing worthy of a sacrifice, I rejected those teachings.

I do not have many beliefs. I prefer to know rather than believe. I do believe in myself – my mind, my abilities and especially the whisperings of The Voice Within for guidance. My path to knowledge is study, reflection, contemplation, reasoning, analysis and above all, unique personal experiences.

We deserve the best that life has to offer. If we ask, seek and knock, the doors will open. We will have the answers we need. It is only a matter of time and the proper "fit" of synchronicities. I asked and what I received was a revelation – cyclic immortality. It explains many of the mysteries.

Let us look at some of these mysteries and find out if we can make sense of them with our new understanding of cyclic immortality.

Here are a few mysteries:

    A. Birth. Where do we come from, if anywhere? Why don't we remember?
    B. Death. Where do we go after we die, if anywhere?
    C. Does life have a purpose?
    D. Why are we attracted or repulsed by certain individuals?
    E. Why do we experience misery, calamities, challenge, pain and suffering? Why evil? Is there justice?
    F. Why sacrifice?

G. Where do our ideas, inspiration and sense of wonder come from?
H. Why do we dream?
I. When babies are born, where do their souls come from? Are there new souls?
J. The mystery of identity. What is self?
K. What exactly is the nature of God?
L. Who are we in relation to God?

BIRTH. WHERE DO WE COME FROM, IF ANYWHERE? WHY DON'T WE REMEMBER?

Each day is a little life: every waking and rising a little birth, every fresh morning a little youth, every going to rest and sleep a little death. – Arthur Schopenhauer

Do we have anything to do with our birth? Or is our birth a chance occurrence? I believe that we choose to be born. Why?

1. To experience beautiful Earth and all that it has to offer: incredible beauty, diversity and unlimited opportunities to experience a range of emotions, feelings and to face challenges as opportunities to gain mastery.
2. To know what it is like to touch, kiss, laugh, cry, scream, hug and relate intimately, deeply and profoundly. There is nothing like it.
3. To interact with others; to develop lifelong friendships and intimacies; to work together; and to love and be loved.
4. To cultivate the higher emotions of empathy, sympathy, understanding, forgiveness, tolerance and inclusivity.

5. To raise our consciousness and to mature into highly effective individuals.
6. To exercise freedom of choice and to experience the consequences of our actions.
7. To discover what we are capable of achieving individually and when working collectively as a unified body of humanity.
8. To solve the mysteries.
9. To wake up to who we are and what we can be.
10. As a way to deal with eternity.

Where Do We Come From? Does life begin with birth? Does an individual's life begin at the moment of conception?

Taking a closer look, we soon realize that all beginnings are illusions. They are convenient points for measurement only. There is no ultimate beginning any more than there is an ultimate ending.

Our lives could not have started at conception or birth. For this to happen, our parents had to exist, meet and marry. Without them we could not have been born. But our parents could not be the starting point of our lives. For our parents to be, their parents had to exist, meet, marry and have children. This line of reasoning continues ad infinitum. Not only did people have to exist to ensure our birth, but earth with its resources had to be in place as well. Without air to breathe, food to eat and water to drink, there can be no life. Everything is interdependent. For earth to be, the sun and the solar system had to be in place as well. This line of reasoning continues indefinitely as well. Since we do not have an ultimate beginning, we cannot have a final end.

So, where is our beginning? Nowhere and everywhere. Any artificial point can serve as a convenient beginning and for this artificial beginning, there is always an equally artificial ending. For all that begins must come to an end. Our birth is an artificial beginning. Our death is an artificial ending. These convenient beginnings and endings are the cycles within eternity.

We come from the other side of the veil and after death we return home. On the spiritual side, there is no beginning or end. There is no birth or death. On the physical side, we begin and we end. We are born and we die. These two sides are the wave of life, the Day and the Night. They make us dual in nature – mortal and immortal, with a beginning and an end physically, and without a beginning or an end spiritually.

WHY DON'T WE REMEMBER WHERE WE CAME FROM?

As you get older three things happen. The first is your memory goes, and I can't remember the other two.   – Norman Wisdom

One early morning, I woke up abruptly around 2:30 am. I knew I had been dreaming, but instantly forgot what the dream was about. I wondered what is the sense of dreaming if we cannot remember the dream? Then, the reason became crystal clear. Waking up is similar to being born. Soon after we are born, we forget where we came from just as, soon after we wake up, we forget what the dream was. The ancients stated this parallel between the two worlds as a law of correspondence – As Above, So Below. Regardless, until the vocal cords and the brain are sufficiently developed, we cannot express ourselves. By the time these are developed, we are fully entrapped in the body adjusting to physical existence, learning and growing. We forget where we came from.

Our birth places us on the stage of life. We must forget our true nature or else we would not enjoy our role. That is why soon after birth, we forget who we truly are, or where we came from. We become actors on the stage of life.

We cannot be successful actors if we constantly "remember" who we truly are. To succeed, we must "forget" our true self and fully assume the role we have accepted to play. For the play to proceed and succeed, we must act out our characters impeccably. We must completely embody our roles.

Where we come from is similar to the dream state. It is real, but not physical. It is a state with its own regulations that are different than the physical ones. There is a good reason why we do not remember where we came from. We remember only what we currently need to live a productive life.

To have an inkling of where we came from, let us take a closer look at our minds. How does an idea manifest? How does a thought appear? How does a word form? These appear "out of nowhere" and just as mysteriously, disappear into the void. In essence we are an idea, a thought, a word in the mind of God. We appear in the mind of God and to it, we return.

Memory is not only conscious. We remember far more than we are aware of. We have subconscious memory, along with many other forms of memory. Our cells remember. Our bodies remember. Lessons learned from painful experiences are never forgotten. These memories remain in the background.

We distill important memories permanently into our character and personality. These we carry from one lifetime to the next. Some of these memories are:

1. Lessons Learned
   a. What works, what does not, what is painful and what is enjoyable
   b. Talents, skills and abilities
   c. People to avoid, others to befriend
2. Family members and acquaintances
3. Preferences for certain foods, cultures, countries

We are inundated with sensory data every moment of our lives. We intentionally forget most of what we sense unless these experiences are judged important. We practice "intentional forgetfulness" when it is advantageous for us to do so. We are not conscious of the trivial in our lives, the routine, or the habitual. The vast majority of our encounters are soon forgotten.

Imagine what would happen if we remembered every license plate we have ever read. Our minds would be cluttered and our brains would become dramatically less efficient. We rarely remember the clothes we wore, the food we consumed, or the subjects we talked about a few days ago. This is intentional. We "forget" where we came from so we can streamline our lives and make them more effective and efficient. Most experiences are mundane and should be forgotten. It must not be important to remember where we came from, hence we forget.

Furthermore, our memories are not reliable. They are selective based on what we pay attention to. These are susceptible to suggestion. We weave stories of our memories and if we repeat them, they become facts even though they are not exactly what took place.

Once born, we forget everything not permanently ingrained in our epi-soul as instinct, character and personality. The body's "operating system" – urges, desires, and passions directed by hormones – take charge. We succumb to physicality, strive to survive, compete and display more of our "bestiality." We forget who we truly are and where we came from until we mature spiritually. Yet a few do remember. They remember their previous lives as documented in several books on the topic of reincarnation. These are exceptions to the general trend.

DEATH. WHERE DO WE GO AFTER WE DIE, IF ANYWHERE?

What we have done for ourselves alone dies with us; what we have done for others and the world remains and is immortal. – Albert Pike

1. The Impetus For Life

Plants are known to grow in cement cracks, on fractured rocks, and even on pavements. There is an impetus to live and survive at any cost. Yet, we age and die. Why?

The other day I accidentally smashed one of my fingers. Instantly the area under my fingernail turned purple and black. My blood vessels were shattered and so were many cells. Promptly, my body began the healing process. In a few months, the finger was back to normal with a new fingernail.

We are exposed to germs continuously. Even when we eat contaminated food or get infected, the body immediately works to restore our health. Yet ultimately, we die. Why?

The question of why we die consumed me for a long time. I could not understand why a species that has been evolving for millions of years still had to experience pain, suffering, aging and death. Eventually I came to the conclusion that if these are our experiences, then these have been selected for the advantages they provide. We experience these not as a punishment or as victims, but rather because we are immortals. These experiences must serve a critical function and they do. We might assume that we die so our species is preserved. Why not preserve the species by avoiding death in the first place? Some would argue that we die to make room for new births and improvement. Why have new births instead of preserving the ones already here?

What advantages do aging and death provide? We die so **we** can be born again with new opportunities to experience and to improve. We die in the old to be born into the new. Death is a respite. We come back fully rested, energized and ready to take on new challenges. We require deadlines to be motivated – death is the ultimate deadline. To experience the pleasure of savoring, we must know hunger. To rest, we must first get tired. To be born anew, we must first die. We die from one drama and are born into a new one, hopefully more exciting.

Once our purpose is fulfilled, we die. We are born with an expiration date. Everything that begins must end. Our sports are timed. We work for a certain number of hours. We sleep for a measured duration. Everything we do is only for a while. So are our lives. This is intentional. This is by choice and through design. Just as in any game, the end must come and the players must stop playing. Yet, the participants do not die. It is only the game that comes to an end. So it is with us. Our life-dramas come to an end, not us as actors. Through rebirth, the players continue to play many more games, hopefully improving with each iteration.

2. The Concept Of Forever And Why We Die

> *Dream as if you'll live forever. Live as if you'll die today.* —James Dean

It is difficult to fathom the concept of "forever". We live by deadlines, end points, and durations. We do not walk forever without aiming to reach someplace. We do not go to school or work without graduation and retirement in our future. Our activities are based on periods. They start and they end. This allows us to enjoy the engagement.

Forever is without time. It never ends. If asked, people would express the desire to live forever **in the same physical body** because they have no idea what "forever" entails. Fear of death and ignorance of what happens after we die force many to cling to life at any cost. We fight death as an archenemy. Even the sick and terminally ill look for ways to stay alive. Obviously, some people commit suicide to escape intolerable situations while others undertake martyrdom so they can go to "heaven." These are exceptions due to extreme duress or fundamental beliefs in a reward after death.

As long as we are uncomfortable with unknowns, we resist death. Once we subconsciously realize that our mission on earth is accomplished, or cannot be and there is nothing else for us to do, we decide to leave. We die. If we resist, then pain, suffering, hopelessness and boredom pave the way. Once the situation becomes intolerable, we let go and we die. No one wants to play the same game forever. No one wants to live in the same place, work at the same job, reside in the same town, and associate with the same people forever. Given a choice, no one wants to be in the same body forever. Eventually, we all must die and we do. This, too, is a choice, albeit, a subconscious one. Death is freedom from the shackles that bind us to sameness. It is our doorway to rebirth and newness.

To ensure that we enjoy life and appreciate our experiences, we live not knowing when we might die. It makes life precious. And when we die, we are gone only for a while to allow for synchronicities to prepare for our next play on the stage of life. We come back renewed and eager to experience life anew having forgotten that we have gone through this numerous times before. This makes life interesting, enjoyable and worthwhile.

3. A New Interpretation Of Resurrection

Every parting is a form of death, as every reunion is a type of heaven. — *Tyron Edwards*

Perhaps there is resurrection after all, not in the same physical body which is impossible, but even better – a brand-new baby body. What can be better than that? A fresh start indeed. We are fortunate beyond measure. This is a gift because we are truly loved. We are resurrected indeed, not once, but over and over. Like a phoenix, we rise from our ashes, in a new body – renewed, rested and ready for a new adventure.

4. Where Do We Go After We Die?

The mind is its own place and in itself, can make a Heaven of Hell, a Hell of Heaven. – John Milton

No one knows the full details of what happens after we die. Some believe that we disintegrate and that is our end – dust to dust. Others believe that we go on to the afterlife where we are judged and either end up in purgatory, heaven or hell. A few who have had near-death experiences believe that they know the answer. These people share their insights: tunnel of light, presence of loved ones, music and beauty. We cannot be sure of the authenticity of these experiences unless we have our own. Until then, the mystery remains.

Perhaps we do not go to a **place** after we die, rather we enter a **state**. The closest similarity to knowing what we experience after death is the state of sleep and dreams. Going to sleep is akin to a small death. Dreaming is similar to after-death experiences. In the dream state, we are free of the limitations of the body, time, space, gravity and the laws of physics. We can go anywhere anytime. We can create to our hearts desire. We can meet with anyone, dead or alive. We experience our true nature unencumbered. Yet, soon after we wake up, we forget these just as we forget where we came from soon after we are born. While our dreams take place in our minds, perhaps our after-death experiences take place in the mind of God. (Law of Correspondence)

We should not fear the unknown, judgement, or dread of oblivion. Our sleeping experiences demonstrate that there is no oblivion. There is however, loss of memory. We need not fear judgement either for a loving God will never judge us for what we did or did not do. Judgement is a human notion and has nothing to do with the nature of a loving and supreme being. How can we have freedom of choice and face judgement at the same time? What we face are the consequences of our actions and inaction, pure and simple.

While plants and animals die naturally, humans, on the other hand, choose and allow it. Being conscious and having free will, we participate in what befalls us. We let go and die because we know, subconsciously or even unconsciously, that it is a mere cycle that we have been through before. The timing of death, however, varies from person to person based on one's purpose, beliefs and circumstances. There are many reasons we might consent to die. You can read about these in the chapter titled: "Understand Why We Age and Die" in my book, **A Passion for Living, a path to meaning and joy**.

Death is not a travesty. Death provides us with unique advantages. Foremost is the ability to cycle through countless lives each providing us with new opportunities. Through death we can start in a new body, and in a totally different environment. Born as babies, we can learn a new language easily and naturally. We learn about and experience new and diverse cultures, and cultivate new acquaintances and friendships.

Death is similar to a natural fire that cleanses and refreshes. An added benefit to death is that it makes our lives temporary. We live, knowing full well that we will die but not knowing when. This makes life precious. Knowing that nothing lasts forever, we take advantage of our circumstances. We act and we make a difference.

Life is precious because it is short. People who know they will die within a short time appreciate their remaining experiences more intensely than those who forget that they could die at any moment.

How much more valuable and meaningful would our time with our beloveds be if we knew that we might never see them again? How much would we savor a meal if we knew that it could be our last? It is the knowledge that we are stamped as "temporary" that makes our connections and relations more meaningful. Uncertainty and a sense of the temporary transform the ordinary into the sublime.

How much more might we appreciate our youth if we remember that we will never be this young again? While young, we tend to forget that we are mortal. We live as if we will never die. However, as we get older, the reality of our situation jolts us into wakefulness. We live with more awareness, especially, when we see acquaintances and loved ones depart without notice. Life is precious because it is temporary.

◆ ◆ ◆

DOES LIFE HAVE A PURPOSE?

He who has a why to live can bear almost any how. — *Friedrich Nietzsche*

Why do we live, some might ask? Is life purposeful, or merely accidental? The answer is simple. All we have to do is look at our lives and at humanity. We have been growing and maturing individually, as a society, as a country, and as a species. We have been growing and maturing physically, mentally, emotionally, socially, technologically, and spiritually.

We are an ecological system. Ecological systems move toward maturity. The march toward maturity is evident everywhere. We see it in our family relations: between husband and wife, parents and their children, siblings and in society. We see it amid employers and employees, among neighbors and between nations.

The purpose of life, therefore, is to experience, to grow and to mature. We are spiritual Alchemists working in the laboratory of earth and physicality in the process of transmuting "lead" into "gold", the crude into the refined, human into the divine.

We live to experience. We experience to grow and build our character and personality. As we do, we sculpt ourselves into a form of our own making. We highlight our individuality. We grow our epi-soul. As our epi-soul grows, we begin to remember who we are and why we are here. We even begin to recollect who we have been in past lives. As we remember, we tap into qualities we developed over previous lifetimes. We actualize more of our potential. We become more aware. Progressively, we attain conscious immortality. We function as co-creators with divinity.

    Maturing is the same as the Seed becoming the Tree, the Image becoming Real, the Idea manifesting as the Word taking Flesh and Dwelling Among us. Once we are mature, we demonstrate love for ourselves, for others, and for nature. Our eyes and our ears open. We begin to SEE without a veil, FEEL without a filter, LISTEN without judgement, and RELATE deeply and intimately. We live as MASTERS manifesting our specialized qualities, individually and collectively.

    Therefore, the ultimate purpose of life is to attain conscious immortality and become partners with God. This is a long and gradual process. This purpose is not imposed on us. It is our natural proclivity. If we have forgotten this purpose, it is because we are asleep to who we are. When we wake up, we will realize that we are living the life we have chosen. Our lives are what we are making of them. Their meaning, value, and purpose are of our own choosing. If we do not see the meaning of our lives, we flounder without a rudder. We succumb to every fad or trend. If, on the other hand, we wake up to our purpose and pursue it, then what we make of ourselves is grand indeed.

    Finally, we should make it part of our purpose to leave our world, the planet and all of its inhabitants, in a better state than when we entered it. This is our duty and obligation. We do not live only for ourselves. Having received, we must give back in return. We are the guardians of our planet.

Life appears without a purpose with its imperfections. This is because we are at an early stage of our growth and unfoldment. As we mature, the purpose of life and our place in it will become crystal clear and self-evident.

◆ ◆ ◆

The March to Maturity

One of the greatest indicators of our own spiritual maturity is revealed in how we respond to the weaknesses, the inexperience, and the potentially offensive actions of others.

—David A. Bednar

As stated, we are alchemists transmuting **lead** into **gold**. The lead in our case is our base emotions, childishness, self-centeredness, ego and immaturity. The gold, on the other hand, is our noble emotions, mature character and developed personality.

Being mature means to calmly handle what life brings our way. It is being prepared and having the confidence that we can manage any given situation. Maturity comes from experience. Like a ripening fruit, we mature slowly and gradually. What is maturing within us is our conscious awareness of who we are, what we are capable of and where we fit in the overall scheme of things. Our consciousness is progressing to greater levels of maturity. Maturity entails the possession of the following qualities:

A. Confidence

Confidence comes from experience. Having been there, done that, and having faced numerable challenges and overcome them, we are prepared and ready. The mature person is fully aware and knows exactly what to do, when to do it, and how.

B. Being At Ease

A mature person does not worry, fret or stress over what is beyond one's control. Maturity brings a sense of calm, peace and serenity that envelops the individual. A mature person does his or her best and accepts the outcome whatever it may be.

C. Knowing What Is Important

Separating the wheat from the chaff. Knowing what is trivial and what is important is a sign of maturity. Most events have no lasting impact and should be ignored. What is important is that which contributes to our well-being, health and happiness, especially in the long run. Cultivating excellent habits, building our character, enhancing our personality, gaining valuable experiences and sharpening our skills are important. So is empowering others and spending time with loved ones.

D. Having Vision (Seeing The Big Picture)

A mature person has vision and does not get mired down in unnecessary details, dramas and distractions. A mature person rises above conflicts and sees the bigger picture. A mature person is in the world but not of the world, and does not contribute to conflict or become part of the problem. If assistance can be rendered, then it is offered. Otherwise, the mature person merely observes, listens, does what is needed and moves on. A mature person can go through "mud" and not get "muddied."

E. Being Unselfish, Considerate And Sympathetic

It is not all about "me". Others are equally important. In fact, for mature people, the focus is often on the other. For it is by serving and enriching the lives of others that personal contentment, satisfaction, and happiness are achieved.

F. Accepting Responsibility For One's Actions And Their Consequences – Living In The Real World

Mature people are responsible. They act instead of react. They do not live in a fantasy world. They see and accept reality as it is. They do not expect that everything will always be rosy. There has to be some ups and downs. There has to be some rainy days to enjoy the sunshine.

And while they are experiencing the sunshine, they prepare for the rain. It is a matter of time before it comes. And while mature people are experiencing hardships, they keep in mind that, "This too shall pass." By going through difficulties and challenges we learn to sympathize with the less fortunate. By having gone through tough times ourselves, we cultivate empathy.

While immature people bully, fight, intimidate and push their way, mature people see the good in the other and find commonality. They create win-win situations. They bring light, peace and harmony wherever they go.

While immature nations prepare for enemies and scheme and plot and go to war to solve their problems, mature nations cooperate, respect others, create partnerships, and undertake joint ventures.

G. Loving, Empowering And Serving

Mature individuals radiate love and a desire to empower. They love others because they can see exactly where these people are. They do not judge because they know that people are doing the best they know under the circumstances. They see others as themselves for they have been there. By seeing others for what they are and loving them for who they are, they empower them.

We have been empowered by the precious gift of free will. We are entitled to live our lives without judgement by the gift giver. By facing the consequences of our actions, we learn, improve and mature. Similarly, as long as they do not infringe on the rights of others, each individual has the right to live their lives as they see fit. They too must be allowed to exercise freedom of choice, face the consequences, learn, improve and mature.

WHY ARE WE ATTRACTED TO OR REPULSED BY CERTAIN INDIVIDUALS?

I suspect the secret of personal attraction is locked up in our unique imperfections, flaws and frailties. – Hugh Mackay

Why are we attracted to some people and not others? Why are we at peace with some, but not others? Is conflict natural? Attraction is often physical and purely biological, yet it is highly specific, why? If we walk into a roomful of people we have never met before, why is it that we might feel attraction to one or two, aversion toward a couple and indifference toward most? What governs our attractions and aversions? If it were a purely biological function, how can we explain the specificity? Even animals are selective when it comes to choosing their mates. What governs choosiness? Obviously, we are attracted to the ones we consider beautiful and are repulsed by those we deem ugly. What governs our considerations? Could it be that it is the memory of our soul? Is it possible that we are born with this memory? Is it conceivable that we have known these people before and these memories linger within our souls?

Who we invite into our lives is not random. Have you ever wondered who your family members are? Why did you fall in love and marry your spouse? Who are your parents? Children? Siblings? Best friends? Acquaintances? Who do you love and who do you have conflict with? Is it possible that we have known each other over eons of time and had previous associations? Is it possible that we have agreed to meet again and play out our dramas in order to help each other grow, overcome challenges and to learn specific lessons? I believe so.

The people in our lives are the ones we need at this time. We attract and bond with them because we "remember" who they are. We interact to resolve conflicts, deepen associations and to rekindle memories of old love. We have known these people from prior lives. They are not strangers. They are often family members in disguise from previous associations.

Why Was Roosevelt Smitten By Martha?

On Sunday April 4, 2021, Public Broadcasting Stations in the Washington DC area began airing "Atlantic Crossing" on Masterpiece. The epic drama is based on the World War II relationship between President Franklin Roosevelt and Norwegian Crown Princess Martha. Martha fled the Nazis with her three young children and lived, for a while, in the White House under Roosevelt's protection.

According to the show, President Roosevelt was taken by Martha at first sight. Was this a coincidence? Is it possible that they had subconscious memories of each other and that they had agreed prior to birth to play out their roles? Franklin's and Martha's relationship was pivotal in turning the tide of WWII. It could not have been accidental.

Often, attraction happens. We do not choose it. It chooses us. This is how it appears outwardly. I do not believe we are victims of circumstance. We are the directors, choreographers and principal actors of all that we participate in. The forces at play are hidden from us. Yet they exist and are the result of our choices and our consent to participate in the ongoing dramas. We are attracted to each other because it is our subconscious desire to do so. We have a purpose to fulfill.

WHY DO WE EXPERIENCE MISERY, CALAMITIES, CHALLENGE, PAIN AND SUFFERING? WHY EVIL? IS THERE JUSTICE?

> *If there were no night, we would not appreciate the day, nor could we see the stars and the vastness of the heavens. We must partake of the bitter with the sweet. There is a divine purpose in the adversities we encounter every day. They prepare, they purge, they purify, and thus they bless.* — James E. Faust

We crave excitement, seek pleasure and love to be euphoric. That is why we have dare devils. While in Auckland, NZ we witnessed our waiter from the cruise ship bungy jump off a tower. Here is a description of that jump:

> "The rush is unbeatable! Leap off the famous Auckland Sky Tower and fall 192 meters straight down. An unforgettable experience for true daredevils, base-jump by wire off the tallest man-made structure in New Zealand."

While we crave excitement consciously, subconsciously we welcome a variety of experiences including misery, calamities, challenge, pain and suffering. In a lifetime, we experience an abundance of feelings and emotions. These provide change, diversion and the means to compare and contrast our various experiences. Some negative encounters are unavoidable. They are part of the human experience. Being eternal, we allow all types of experiences into our lives. Some people, after going through pain and suffering become creative – writing and singing beautiful melodies.

1. Misery

> *I am determined to be cheerful and happy in whatever situation I may find myself. For I have learned that the greater part of our misery or unhappiness is determined not by our circumstance but by our disposition.*
>
> – Martha Washington

Why are so many people unhappy? Healthy, happy, successful people are the exception. The vast majority of the human population are living in squalor. If humanity is like a pyramid, most would be in a support mode for the few elites and fortunate ones at the top.

Health, happiness and success are possible, yet they elude most. Why? If individuals discover, develop and excel at what they are passionate about and follow the promptings of The Voice Within, they will at least be comfortable and content, if not fully healthy, happy and successful. This does not usually happen. Why?

We are constantly fighting against "entropy". In our case, status quo and stagnation. It takes effort to be self-motivated, to seek, to excel, to develop talents, skills and specialized abilities. Many prefer the road most travelled, requiring the least effort. They accept their fate as destiny, the will of God or misfortune.

I believe there is another reason. Is it possible that we recycle our roles in the various positions of society? One lifetime being the "Chief" and several other lifetimes being the "Indian." Each position affords us different opportunities to develop needed skills and abilities. Hence, is it possible that those who are leaders today will play support roles next time around, and those at the bottom will rise higher? This is akin to the penguins in Antarctica during winter where they huddle together to stay warm, but continuously alternate who is inside the circle and who is at the periphery. This way everyone experiences the cold and the warmth. Since there are many more positions at the bottom of the pyramid than at the top, most find themselves at the bottom rung of the pyramid of life. Be heartened, though. All positions are temporary with expiration dates. Our chance will come to occupy new positions. Next time, we might be at the top. We must, however, prepare for these positions and qualify. Failures, misery, challenges, difficulties, pain and suffering are excellent ways to prepare and to qualify for loftier positions in this life and in lives to come.

2. Calamities

> *He who knows no hardships will know no hardihood. He who faces no calamity will need no courage. Mysterious though it is, the characteristics in human nature which we love best grow in a soil with a strong mixture of troubles.*
> – Harry Emerson Fosdick

Why Do We Experience Calamities?

As I write this, several states are experiencing the calamitous effects of Hurricane Ida. Many died or lost their homes with widespread destruction. Just as we go through cycles, so does planet Earth. Nature is mostly predictable, but not always. We wake up every day expecting it to be like any other day. We get used to routine. We are lulled into complacency. We stop being vigilant. Living is exposure to the unpredictable. It is the unpredictability of life that keeps us on our toes. The reality is, we do not know what might happen in any instant. Life is a drama, but not everything is pre-planned. There is quite a lot of improvisation. Like any game, life is unpredictable. Unpredictability provides excitement, anticipation and hopefully, vigilance. What we consider a calamity could be the genesis of change that leads to an ever-enhanced quality of life. The measure of an event is not always the immediate effects it has, but rather, the long-term consequences resulting from that event.

What we consider "good" today might not end up being good in the long run. Similarly, what we term as "bad or calamitous" might carry within it the seeds of progress, renewal and the genesis of higher consciousness. The evolution of our consciousness necessitates that we experience "calamities" every once in a while. We require failures and hardships to grow. Calamities provide opportunities for us to help each other, make us stronger and, over time, wiser as well.

The cycles of life embrace calamities, including death and destruction. These have a role to play in the overall scheme of things. Earthquakes, volcanoes and droughts cause incredible damage both to human life and the ecosystem. Yet they can lead to some benefits as well. We can learn to appreciate nature, design and build better communities, prepare and be ready. We can stockpile necessities during abundant harvests in preparation for a drought, as the ancient Egyptians did. Wild fires might be calamitous. Yet they burn the debris, rejuvenate and invigorate the landscape. Rainstorms drench the landscape refilling our reservoirs. Surgery is painful, but it can lead to healing. Where there is calamity, there is the opportunity to volunteer, to lend a hand and to shine. The ups and downs of life ultimately balance each other. While predators keep the prey in check and allow for the improvement of the species, humans have no predators. They only have nature to play that role. Natural disasters, diseases, and calamities keep us on our toes. They expose us to our weaknesses and shortcomings. They force us to reconsider our ways. They are our "predators." And just as predators are not the enemies of the prey, neither are calamities. Death and destruction are horrible. In the final analysis, death in one life time is not an annihilation. We come back fresh and ready. If we suffer calamities in one life time, perhaps we will avoid them next time around. We take turns. No one is privileged more than another. In the long run, everything balances out. Everyone experiences ups and downs.

3. Challenge

> *You should never view your challenges as a disadvantage. Instead, it's important for you to understand that your experience facing and overcoming adversity is actually one of your biggest advantages.*   – Michelle Obama

Personal challenges are opportunities to overcome and gain mastery of the situation. By overcoming our challenges, we grow. We enhance our self-esteem, polish our character and personality, and we set an example for others to follow.

National and international challenges are also opportunities to "grab the bull by the horn" and make a positive contribution. They are occasions to demonstrate the quality of our character. Do we cave in or do we face and resolve our challenges? Do we act with fairness or do we take advantage of the situation for personal gain?

The Israeli and Palestinian conflict is a protracted international challenge. It is an opportunity for creative resolution of a problem that appears intractable. Solutions are always available, yet they might not be where we are looking but rather just around the corner. In this case, we have a powerful nation that can impose its will through might. On the other side is a population of humans who have no recourse to any meaningful resistance. What is the solution? It rests with the powerful. The powerful have an opportunity to either continue to oppress the weak or to act with compassion, understanding and benevolence. Realizing that those who are the rulers in this lifetime can easily be the ruled in the next, should propel us to treat others equitably and with respect. We are all humans prone to pain and suffering. We are also capable of transcending our lower nature and rising to new heights of benevolence, compassion, fairness and justice. Who we consider to be "our people" can easily expand to include others. What separates us is far less than what we have in common. We need to open, not only our eyes, but our hearts as well. Everyone benefits when problems are resolved and when peace, harmony and cooperation are the norm.

4. Pain And Suffering

The climb might be tough and challenging, but the view is worth it. There is a purpose for that pain; you just can't always see it right away.

– Victoria Arlen

It is not difficult to understand why we experience pain and suffering. We are not as rational as we think. We are more emotional beings than we realize. Often, we require pain and suffering to learn critical life lessons. We also attribute value to effort. If we do not pay for something, it is often not valued. Pain and suffering are what we pay to learn important life lessons. If we make a mistake and the pain that results is negligible, chances are, we will repeat our mistake. Once the price we pay is high enough emotionally, it registers and we learn. We might neglect our bodies until we are forced to reconsider through a painful incident. If pain and suffering did not have intrinsic value, they would cease to exist and would be "de-selected" out of our lives. We can live intelligently and avoid unnecessary pain and suffering. We do not have to make a mistake and learn from it. We can live preventive lives and avoid most mistakes. We can also learn from the pain of others, especially those who are suffering.

5. Why Evil?

> *The only thing necessary for the triumph of evil is for good men to do nothing.*
>
> *– Edmund Burke*

There are at least three ways to look at why evil exists.

1. Evil is perpetrated by immature souls who are mostly new, childlike and selfish. They are usually new to planet Earth.
2. Evil exists as an opportunity for us to con-

front it, take action, and implement necessary changes so we can grow and mature.
3. The evil perpetrators might be playing out agreed upon roles and are not evil in themselves. We play different roles to pave the way for dramas to unfold and events to take place so end results can be achieved.

Even though evil exists, its impact is temporary. Triumph over evil is permanent and glorious. While God personifies "Good", the Devil personifies "Evil." While God resides in "Heaven", the Devil resides in "Hell." As agents of change, it is our job to transform hell into heaven.

6. Is There Justice?

There really can be no peace without justice. There can be no justice without truth. And there can be no truth, unless someone rises up to tell you the truth. – Louis Farrakhan

Recently a mother in California lost her 6-year-old son to road rage. He was shot and the assailant fled. The mother pleaded for help in apprehending the assailant so justice could be served. But how can there ever be justice if she can never recover her child? The only justice is for the assailant to experience the consequences of his or her actions. That can only happen if the assailant is a mother next time around and experiences the loss of a child. This can only happen through cyclic immortality. Enter karma, the gateway to true justice.

On Wednesday, June 16, 2021 the Washington Post published an article headlined: "Billionaire gives hundreds of millions to another surprising list of colleges." The billionaire is MacKenzie Scott, one of the world's wealthiest people who was married to Amazon founder Jeff Bezos from 1993 to 2019.

Imagine a similar scenario – a female grows up and ends up marrying one of the wealthiest people in the country and another female born in a very poor country, ends up homeless on the streets. Where is the justice in this?

Cyclic immortality makes justice possible. We take turns playing various roles. In one lifetime, we can be the girl on the streets and in another, we can be the fortunate wealthy. More important than wealth and poverty is the realization that these are circumstances with hidden opportunities. What we do with what we are dealt is the critical factor. Do we maximize the benefits of wealth and make a positive difference in the world like MacKenzie Scott did? Or do we squander this opportunity? Similarly, do we take advantage of our situation as homeless and learn about the poor and the hopeless? Do we resolve to do something constructive with our lives even under these circumstances? Keep in mind that all experiences are opportunities to learn from and to grow through. Instead of complaining about our situation and the absence of justice, we should focus on what we can do in the given situation. Justice is always served, but only in the long haul over many lifetimes.

When I first read the Parable of the Talents, I wondered why the master gave different talents to each of his servants. Why 1, 5 and 10 talents? Where is the justice in that? Did they have different abilities? How come?

I believe this parable is allegorical. Initially, we each receive one talent. As we live, some of us invest wisely and add to our talent, perhaps doubling it and our one talent becomes two. In the next life, some do even better, increasing their talents from two to five. A few are exceptional and over a few life cycles end up with ten talents. Hence, there is no injustice in what we end up with. We all start with one. What we do with our one talent makes all the difference. The same way that we start each day with 24 hours. It is what we do in those 24 hours that separates us one from another. Do we invest? Or, do we squander our precious time? We are expected to at least double what we start with in each life. We must put our "talents" to productive use, not bury them in the ground as if they do not exist.

"For it will be like a man going on a journey, who called his servants and entrusted to them his property. To one he gave five talents, to another two, to another one, to each according to his ability. Then he went away. He who had received the five talents went at once and traded with them, and he made five talents more. So also he who had the two talents made two talents more. But he who had received the one talent went and dug in the ground and hid his master's money. Matt 25:14-18

Justice does not pertain only to law, but individual circumstances as well. Imagine a mother with several children she cannot adequately care for. Envision her living a short, miserable life and then passing away. Where is the justice in that? Justice is for her to have an opportunity for a better life next time around. In a future life, she might shun having many children and focus instead on enjoying her life. Perhaps, her next lifetime will be a vacation. Justice is served.

Imagine a father in a similar situation. Out of desperation with his lot in life, he becomes abusive. Wouldn't he want another chance for a new life where he has the opportunity to amend his mistakes and make up for his bad behavior? Cyclic immortality avails him of such an opportunity. Justice is served.

Imagine making a terrible blunder. Being sorry is never enough. The damage is done. We need another opportunity to make up for what we did. Cyclic immortality provides us with such an opportunity. Through cyclic immortality, if we are a failure in this life, we would have an opportunity for success in the next one. If we are poor this life time, we have an opportunity to be wealthy in the next. If we are weak this time, we will have a chance to be strong next time around. Only cyclic immortality, over time, guarantees equal opportunity, fairness and justice for all.

7. WHY SACRIFICE?

> *Life is a song - sing it. Life is a game - play it. Life is a challenge - meet it. Life is a dream - realize it. Life is a sacrifice - offer it. Life is love - enjoy it.*
> —Sai Baba

I clearly remember how moved I was when I read, **A Tale of Two Cities** by Charles Dickens. The narrative suggests that Sydney Carton's self-sacrifice secures a new, peaceful life for Lucie Manette. The idea that love, at times, requires sacrifice is in Christianity as well.

> *"For God so loved the world, that he gave his only Son, that whoever believes in him should not perish but have eternal life. For God did not send his Son into the world to condemn the world, but in order that the world might be saved through him.*   John 3:16-17

We call those who sacrifice their lives for others, heroes. Why does anyone, knowingly, sacrifice their life for another?

Individuals sacrifice their lives for the benefit of others because deep down they know that their lives do not end with death. If death were the end of it all, we would have been biologically prevented from sacrificing our lives for others. The knowledge that death is not the end comes from deep within. It is instinctive. Perhaps we sacrifice our lives for others, knowing deep down, that either someone in the past sacrificed his or her life for us or perhaps in a future life, someone else will do the same for us. We are connected in more ways than we realize.

Not all sacrifices are conscious and willful. I strongly believe that my mother sacrificed her life for the sake of her children. My mother was 36 years old when she passed away, leaving 6 children behind. We were in Aleppo, Syria living in squalor, extremely poor and without any hope of a better life. My father could not care for us even while my mother lived. After her death, he was forced to scatter us hoping we would have a chance for a better life. He ordered the eldest son out to be on his own, placed three in orphanages and sent me to a monastery in Lebanon. He kept one with him. Had my dad died instead of my mother, we would never have left Syria. We would have had no hope of a better future. With her death and our placements, we were on our way to freedom and a better chance at life. My mother's death was a sacrifice indeed. A sacrifice of love albeit, unconscious. By sacrificing for each other we avail people opportunities they would otherwise never have. In the long run, everyone wins.

> *I am a member of a team, and I rely on the team, I defer to it and sacrifice for it, because the team, not the individual, is the ultimate champion.*   – Mia Hamm

How do we reconcile self-sacrifice and the instinct to survive?

7. WHY SACRIFICE? | 155

The traditional view of evolution is that it is based on natural selection and survival of the fittest. Through selective advantageous traits, the species not only survives but thrives. Evolution is not concerned with individuals but rather the survival of the species. How can evolution, a blind force, differentiate between survival of individuals and that of the species? How can the species survive if individuals do not survive? I understand evolution to be directed by consciousness. That is why the instinct for survival and self-sacrifice can coexist. Our soul, imbued with consciousness, allows individual sacrifice for the welfare of the species.

Survival is a primal instinct, yet there is an equally powerful instinct – mating and reproduction through which survival of the species is secured. Male animals go to extreme lengths to compete and have access to females. Human males have an equally strong urge to have access to females. Why is mating and reproduction an overarching desire? It is so we can continue to be born again and again and undergo earthly experiences as a way to manage our immortality. How else can we explain individual sacrifice for its species? If the species survive, we can continue to be reborn.

Our mating hormones (testosterone and estrogen) are strongest when we are most fit to reproduce and care for our offspring. That is why our hormones are "programmed" to wane as we age. Why else?

Plants and animals have an innate urge to survive and reproduce because we depend on them for our survival. If plants and animals do not survive, we do not survive. Hence, the interconnected web of life. Just as there are "key species" in nature that are critical for the survival of others, humans are the ultimate "key species." If we do not survive, nothing else matters.

WHERE DO OUR IDEAS, INSPIRATION, AND SENSE OF WONDER COME FROM?

1. Ideas/Inspiration

Great minds discuss ideas; average minds discuss events; small minds discuss people.

– Eleanor Roosevelt

Like fiber optics that carry multiple independent bands, various realities coexist in the same space/time differing in their vibratory rates. At the two extremes are the physical world and the spiritual state. "Somewhere" in between these two, is an "other worldly" reality where our entire past and present are stored and future potentialities are available. This world is a living video library of all that has ever happened, is happening and can ever take place. It houses all ideas and is the source of all inspirations. It is also the wellspring of inventions, breakthroughs, visions, gut feelings, and extra-sensory perceptions. Perhaps this is what the ancients alluded to when they spoke of the Akashic Records. Our Higher Self is connected to this "other world." When we ascend the ladder of consciousness, or somehow detach from this reality, we can "touch" this world. The information stored there becomes available to us.

The first time I experienced this state was when I was working as a waiter in a resort in the mountains of Lebanon aptly named "Shangri-La". I was in the kitchen downstairs when a young employee came running through the kitchen chased by my supervisor who asked me to grab the running employee and restrain him. I did. The employee was fired and his dad blamed me for the incident. The next day I was told to hide in the hotel and not come out for a few days because the dad was out with a gun looking to kill me. I was frightened because the dad was an uneducated villager who took matters into his own hands to settle disputes. He was determined to avenge his son's firing. I was in hiding and mulling over my situation when suddenly I entered a world where I was a mere witness. It was as if a video recording was playing what was to unfold. In a vision, I saw in detail the father with the gun and what would happen if I ventured out. I "saw" that the fury will subside in a couple of days and that I should wait it out.

What was strange about this incident is the state I found myself in. I was "trapped" in a state where I could only observe. I had no ability to speak, act or participate. I was watching a movie of what would happen if I ventured out.

The second time I entered this state was prior to my Near-Death Experience where I witnessed my funeral in detail. I describe this incident in my book, **A Passion for Living, a path to meaning and joy.**

    I am inspired frequently. I regularly wake up in the middle of the night with an explanation, an insight, or an inspired thought that is in support of what I am focused on at the time – the answer I need. I have gotten up repeatedly to write these answers down as they came, at times, every 10 or 15 minutes. The answers come, seemingly "out of the blue", yet they are pertinent and on target.

    When we seriously ask, seek and knock, we "charge and magnetize" our consciousness. We consciously create a "seed" with an explicit task. This seed becomes like a puzzle missing a key part. When we release this seed into our subconscious mind which is in touch with our Higher Self, it seeks the missing part – the answer we need. Our Higher Self is in touch with this "other world" and all worlds. Once the answer is found, it is presented to us at an opportune time. This is how I am inspired. It happens frequently. In fact, this is how I get the answers I need and how I write my books. Like Prometheus, my Higher Self touches this "other world" and "steals the fire from the gods" and presents it to me as a gift – the answer I need.

2. Sense Of Wonder

Life never becomes a habit to me. It's always a marvel.
— Katherine Mansfield

Have you ever been "struck" by beauty? I have, more than once. Have you ever listened to a song, read a book and were touched to your core? Have you ever watched a movie or listened to a story and were overwhelmed by emotion? Has a fleeting moment ever left an indelible impression in your heart? If you have, then you have experienced the sublime. While the body experiences emotions such as pain and pleasure, fear and anger, all of which are ordinary; the soul experiences wonder, joy, beauty and divine love, all of which are transcendent and sublime.

We appear to be biologically wired to experience the sublime. We are born into and live with a sense of connection to the sublime and to a reality higher than our individual selves. The sense of the sublime comes from the depth of our being. It is the yearning of our soul to connect with a reality beyond the physical, a reality that is our source and destination. This reality manifests in moments of inspiration, insight, and through unusual experiences. In my book, **A Passion for Living, a path to meaning and joy,** I describe a simple experience I once had while eating an ordinary garden tomato that turned out to be anything but ordinary. This experience transformed my life.

Our earthly experiences provide us many opportunities to touch the sublime. The birth of a child, sunrise and sunset, touch, intimacy, communion, and even simple everyday experiences can be sublime: walking, talking, singing, dancing, even enjoying a meal or a cup of tea with a beloved. Radiating love, appreciating beauty, exuding joy and experiencing wonder are a failproof recognition of the sublime within us. Without the sublime, we will be just as the beasts are – competing and struggling to exist. Because we have the sublime within – soul, we can recognize the sublime without.

WHY DO WE DREAM?

I dreamed I was a butterfly, flitting around in the sky; then I awoke. Now I wonder: Am I a man who dreamt of being a butterfly, or am I a butterfly dreaming that I am a man? –Zhuzngzi

Are dreams random activities of the brain, or are they a reflection of a far greater reality than what is apparent? Dreams are complex and simple explanations cannot do them justice. If we keep a dream journal for a long time, we will realize that dreams are the way our body and our Higher Self communicate symbolically with us. Dreams give us a glimpse of how we would function out of the body. They also make it clear that we are of two worlds: Physical (Earth) and non-physical (Heaven). While we are in the body, we are confined and obey physical laws. Out of the body, we are unencumbered and follow a different set of rules.

Everyone dreams. Even though most of our dreams are forgotten, we do remember some of them every once in a while. Many dreams appear to be trivial in nature and can easily be dismissed. These can be attributed to diet, worries, medications, bodily sensations and brain activity. A few remain inexplicable and puzzling. These involve our Higher Self. An example of this is lucid dreaming. Some lucid dreams are more vivid than wakeful reality. I have had several of these.

My first one occurred when I was about 16 years old. It was so vivid and detailed that it has stayed with me until today. Some details in lucid dreams are new information. They are not from memory or previous experiences, but can be verified later on.

Another type of dream that is a communication from our Higher Self is a prophetic dream (premonition). I have had some of these as well. In one dream, I was having a conversation with my supervisor. However, upon waking up, I completely "forgot" the dream. While at work several hours later my supervisor called me to her office. As I was conversing with her, suddenly I remembered my dream. Our conversation was word for word from my dream that morning.

Dreams have a great impact on our moods. On the morning of 9/22/2021, I woke up full of energy, excitement and eager to work. This is because of a delightful lucid dream. Similarly, the effects on people who dream of departed loved ones are lasting and the information exchanged is comforting and reassuring. It can even lead to inspiration. Here is an example:

> *Who Was "Mother Mary"?*
>
> *Alluded to in the lyrics to "Let It Be," Mary wasn't – as widely thought – ever meant to be the Virgin or Mary Magdalene. Rather, it was McCartney's own mother, Mary, who died of cancer when he was 14. He got the idea for the song after having a dream about her. (Parade, Sunday, October 24, 2021)*

It is fascinating to delve into the nature of dreams. The deeper we wade into our dreams, the more amazed we become. There is much more to dreams than meets the eye. Dreams show us that we are more than a physical body trapped in space and time. In our dreams, we leave behind not only our bodies, but also the constraints of space, time, the spoken word, our age, sex, nationality, and our current reality. Dreams are a window into our true nature and a reflection of the limitless self that we are. Dreams take us into a fantasy world. They stimulate and strengthen our imagination, give us hope and provide answers we need. Could dreams also be an indication that we live parallel lives?

In our dreams we move, communicate, and act. While dreaming, we believe that in fact we are doing all these things. Once we wake up, however, we realize that we have never left our bed. It has all been an illusion. Our powerful minds create the circumstances we experience in our dreams including the illusion of space/time and motion. Could this be the same for our wakeful reality? Could our wakeful activities be taking place in the mind of God?

Even though dream events appear illusory, it does not mean that the events did not take place or that they are insignificant. They are real where they happen, in their particular dimension. Dreams are real while we dream them. Physical experiences are real while we are awake and fully aware of our activities. Both dreams and physical experiences take place in the same mind. While dreams are symbolic, physical experiences are literal.

Have you ever wondered why the last book in the New Testament is called Revelations? Nothing is revealed there. In fact, that book is so confusing that hardly anyone understands it. This is because the book is a vision, a dream, completely symbolic.

To better understand the symbolic nature of our dreams, we must think of them as personal plays or dramas. Even though we remember only snippets of dreams, they can reveal their meaning never-the-less. Dreams are a reflection of what is going on in our lives. Dreams can mix various events to create a drama. This symbolic message might or might not be clear.

Here are some questions to consider:

1. What is the theme or the idea behind the dream?
2. Assuming that a dream is a play or a drama, what message is it conveying?
3. How can we describe the theme in one or two words?
4. What are some other words or phrases that express the same idea?
5. Who or what situation does this theme reference? What person or situation embodies the theme?
6. How does this dream relate to what is happening in our lives?
7. Did we read or hear an unusual piece of information or news related to the theme of the dream?
8. Did we lose, receive or give something related to the theme of the dream?
9. Did we watch a movie the night before that might have impacted us?
10. Did we hear or see something that causes us stress and worry?

As an example, I have been having a recurring dream. In these dreams, I have an urgent need to urinate. I am frantically looking for a rest room. I am scurrying from place to place trying to locate a bathroom that I can use. Either I cannot find one, or the ones I locate are filthy or occupied. Ultimately, I find a primitive bathroom way out of the way.

What is the theme of these dreams in one or two words? **Release.** I am holding onto something I need to release. Letting go is another way to describe this theme. I must let go. Let go of what? If we think about it, we will come to realize what it is that we are not letting go of. Dreams are symbolic communications. We must heed their messages. If releasing is difficult, the dream will recur until the release is complete. Some recurring dreams could also be a message from the body about an impending malady if we refuse to release and let go.

Here is an example where anxiety, worry, fear, desire and belief translate into mini-dramas as dreams.

I am at work. Before I go home, I stop at a store and purchase a few items. I want to take the Metro home, but one item is too large to take on the Metro. I decide to call my wife and ask her to come and pick me up. However, I am unable to locate her icon on my phone to speed dial her number. I look again and again to no avail. I cannot remember her number to use the number pad. I begin to stress. I feel stuck not knowing what to do. That is when I wake up.

After reflecting on the dream, the meaning became clear. A week ago, I had purchased a new smart phone. I got everything to work properly except for my email. I could not figure out how to send or receive emails. Hence the reason for my dream with a transference of the malfunction from email to a phone number.

Here is another recent dream with its symbolic meaning:

I am with two African American males. They look alike.

"Are you twins?" I asked one of them.

"Twins?" the other replied. "We are not even alike. Can't you see the scar on his face. I do not have a scar."

"But the scar is incidental", I said. "It is not part of him."

What is the meaning of this dream? It is about two individuals: another and me. Perhaps subconsciously, I believe that I am different or better than the other because of a scar on another's face that is obvious to see. A scar is a blemish due to an undesirable behavior. The message of the dream is for me to understand that even though we appear different on the surface, fundamentally, we are the same, practically identical twins. Scars are not permanent. They are not identifying marks. They are temporary and will fade with time.

WHEN BABIES ARE BORN, WHERE DO THEIR SOULS COME FROM? ARE THERE NEW SOULS?

Make no mistake about why these babies are here - they are here to replace us.   *– Jerry Seinfeld*

Babies are born continuously. They do not have new souls. The same souls are being reborn. Hence, souls are not "created" with each baby. The concept of "number of souls" is linear. Soul, being multi-dimensional and quantum, is beyond linearity, space and time. The same soul can manifest in numerous individuals each having their own unique experiences.

Mind is always a "pregnant potentiality for ideas." An idea, even when expressed, never "literally" leaves the mind. What is expressed is a "semblance" of the idea. All souls originate in the mind of God as ideas. While in the mind of God, unmanifest and unbound, the soul of each individual is known as the **Higher Self**. Once expressed, "the idea becomes the word, takes flesh, and dwells among us." It becomes our individual soul with two components: basic soul and epi-soul. Basic soul is always the same while the epi-soul is specific for that particular lifecycle.

Once expressed, ideas become individualized with unique identities. Potentially, an idea can express itself in numerous ways. For example, the idea of a book can be expressed in any language and in any format. The number of copies made of an expressed idea, such as a book, are limitless. Furthermore, the idea of a book is only one form of an idea. The mind can generate limitless ideas.

The Higher Self can never occupy a physical body. It is massive and powerful with unlimited capabilities. What descends into the baby, is a small "package" specifically designed for what is needed for that particular life. Each of us is born with basic soul as our identity and a specific packaging of epi-soul perfect for what we will need for our earthly experience. While basic soul remains intact, we are expected to use our epi-soul productively and add to it.

Being born is like going on a journey. On any journey, there is us and our suitcase. The "us" is our basic soul. Our "suitcase" is our epi-soul, a specific packaging for the journey we are undertaking. If our trip is short, we take less with us than if we are cruising around the world. Each trip has a purpose. For example, if we are going skiing, what we take with us is geared toward skiing.

We never take our entire belongings or assets with us on any journey. We prepare a suitcase specific for our upcoming trip. We take enough money for what we believe we might require. The rest of our belongings stay at home and most of our money remains in the bank. Our Higher Self is our home and the bank. It houses all of our "spiritual capital" accumulated over eons of living, experiencing and learning. If while on our trip we require more assets, we can access our Higher Self and request what we need.

To access our Higher Self, we need to climb "Jacob's Ladder." We do this through prayer, meditation and the employment of our higher emotions. The good news is that our Higher Self is in contact with all other Higher Selves. If we need something we do not have, we can get it from whoever has it. This is how inspiration, breakthroughs and innovations take place. This is how we receive the answers we seek.

THE MYSTERY OF IDENTITY. WHAT IS SELF?

1. The Ego

Don't let your ego get too close to your position, so that if your position gets shot down, your ego doesn't go with it. – Colin Powell

Wikipedia defines ego as: "*that portion of the human personality which is experienced as the "self" or "I" and is in contact with the external world through perception.*" The ego is who we are physically, socially and in the eyes of others. The ego is what we are in this lifetime. It is the superficial way we distinguish one individual from another. The ego is an illusion. It is due to genetics, environment and circumstance in one lifetime. It does not define us. While on earth, we are intricately connected to all else. We do not have a separate individuality. Separation is a mirage. We are not only intricately linked to all other living beings, but we are also inseparable from nature. If we do not breathe, eat and drink, and interact with our environment, we will cease to exist.

In essence, we are all the same. We appear different because we assume temporal and mortal existence. In each lifetime, we take on a different role and thus appear and act differently. Yet these roles are not our essence. Just as actors revert back to their original selves once the play is over, so do we upon leaving the body at death.

Differences are superficial. Even though some are poor while others are rich and even though some are beautiful while others appear not to be, and even though some are highly intelligent while others do not seem to be, in essence, we are all the same. Differences are the "costumes and makeup" we put on. This is so the "drama" of life can go on. Imagine putting on a play and having all actors be the same. In any drama, play, or game, variety in the roles played is a necessity but only during the performance. Once the game is over and we are on the other side, we celebrate together as co-equals.

According to science, environment and heredity determine individuality. These two alone do not adequately explain differences between people. Family members often share a great deal of heredity and environment, yet exhibit distinct personality traits. Two children born to the same parents and living under identical circumstances can exhibit incredibly different traits and personalities at an early age. I believe that a third factor is required to explain differences in people – "epi-soul." Epi-soul is what we build in each life time. It contains our accumulated experiences and the memories of lessons learned. It is what distinguishes us from each other as distinct personalities.

Deep inside, we know that we are more than genetics and environment. We are a soul personality (epi-soul) with inherited memories, talents and abilities from several past lives. The arena of life is a trinity of forces – our epi-soul, genetics, and environment. These three interact and in the process, all are changed. We influence our genes and our environment and in the process are shaped by them. Of the three, we are the most influential, for we can modify not only our external environment, but greatly influence our internal environment as well. We do this by carefully choosing our thoughts, feelings, beliefs, attitudes, and expectations. We can even influence our genetics through intent, visualization and meditation.

2. The True Self

> *People often say that this or that person has not yet found himself. But the self is not something one finds; it is something one creates.*
>
> *– Thomas Szasz*

The confusion between who we are and what we are is prevalent. We are not our bodies. We are a living soul. We have bodies. We live in the body for a specific duration and then we move on.

We are on the stage of life. We don the appropriate costumes and put on the makeup that reflects our roles as actors. Antagonisms, fights, disputes, alliances, and conflicts are merely parts of the drama, put on to create anticipation, excitement and to enhance the drama. However, once the curtain falls, the game ends, and we die, the costumes and makeup come off and the roles are shed. We revert back to who we really are – beings of light. While we appear different on the stage of life, on the other side of the veil, we are all the same.

We are not our bodies or the roles we assume. **We are soul.** Soul is what allows us to experience the transcendent, appreciate beauty, enjoy the arts, soar with music, be moved by noble deeds and even sacrifice ourselves for others. Our soul is the sublime within. It is inseparable from God. As such, our true identity is of the nature of God. It is sublime and divine. Like God, our true self is characterized by a trinity of sublimes:

1. Love
2. Beauty
3. Joy

Experiencing love, beauty and joy is witnessing our essence in action. Exuding joy is how we feel when we encounter beauty and love. Being love, we see beauty and experience joy everywhere. Being love, appreciating beauty and experiencing joy is manifesting our divinity. It is expressing our true nature – a trinity of sublimes: Love, Beauty and Joy.

WHAT EXACTLY IS THE NATURE OF GOD?

Sir, my concern is not whether God is on our side; my greatest concern is to be on God's side, for God is always right. – Abraham Lincoln

The vast majority of the people on the planet believe in God. Theories regarding the nature of God abound. Everyone has an understanding or a belief of who and what God is. What we believe is important for it guides our lives. Ultimately, regardless of our beliefs, what matters most is not what we believe, but rather what we know for a fact and how we live expressing our beliefs.

For many, God is Love. This is a beautiful and a wonderful concept. However, what exactly does this mean? Mostly, different things to different people. Yet, for those who have experienced deep and profound spiritual love, the nature of God is self-evident. No need for theories. They know God is Love because they have experienced true love themselves.

To be love is not the same as being in love or loving someone. Those who fall in love can fall out of love as well. Spiritual love is different. It transcends space and time. It is absolute. In this love, the concept of selfhood dissolves. We no longer see the beloved as a mere person, but rather as a divine personification of God. The overwhelming joy that comes from loving spiritually and being love is the best indicator of the nature of God.

Belief without action is dead.

For as the body apart from the spirit is dead, so also faith apart from works is dead.   James 2:26

Expressing our beliefs in action is powerful and transformative. I view God as a trinity of Love, Beauty and Joy. Being love, appreciating beauty and exuding joy personifies, demonstrates and manifests God.

WHO ARE WE IN RELATION TO GOD?

It is love that brings individuals together and propels them to form a larger group, a mastermind assembly. Love is the innate realization that whenever two or more come together in love, new benefits will be realized by all. This innate realization is the driving force behind cell division and our innate desire to reproduce. This innate force that ever propels us to join and unite manifests as desire, attraction, lust and love. Because of this innate force, life can progress, unfold and mature.
– A Passion for Living, a path to meaning and joy

Imagine a sphere with God at the center. God radiates Love, Beauty and Joy as wave emanations. As the wave spreads out, it gets further from the center, its source, and becomes attenuated. Hence, those closest to the center are most godlike – Love, Beauty and Joy. As the wave spreads out, it slows down and becomes progressively denser. Those farthest from the center are least God-like.

Those closest to God are the spiritual beings. Next come humans, then animals, plants and finally the mineral kingdom. We are first in line as embodied beings. Because we have free will, how we relate to God is personal. The intent is for us to be **partners with God.**

The best partnerships are when those involved are bound together by love and a common purpose. Even though we might not know how to love our partner – God, God's love for us, as partners, is beyond measure; so much so that God gave us a most precious gift – freedom of choice to do with as we please. We are on Earth to live freely and gradually discover our role in this partnership. We do this through trial and error, pain and suffering, and pleasure and joy. Once we mature in our relationship, we become part of a mastermind group. A healthy, vibrant human body is a perfect example of a mastermind group. Each cell in the body is independent, yet functioning in awareness and cooperation with all other cells. Each tissue functions at its optimum. Each organ does its job to perfection and each system contributes its best for the welfare of the entire body. As emanations from God, it is our destiny to evolve and assume our roles as full partners with God – participants in creation and the evolution of consciousness.

(For a detailed description of the mastermind concept, please refer to my book, **A Passion for Living, a path to meaning and joy.)**

PART V

Making the Most of the Revelation

MAKING THE MOST OF THE REVELATION

The greatest revelation of my generation is that a human being can alter his life by altering his attitudes. — William James

If we know that smoking can ruin our health and we still smoke, do we really know? The benefit of knowledge is in its application. To derive the most advantage from the revelation of cyclic immortality, we must incorporate knowledge into our life philosophy. It must be what we believe, know and live. To make the most of the revelation, we must:

    A. Understand the nature of life
    B. Make the most of this life
    C. Plan our next life

UNDERSTAND THE NATURE OF LIFE

Nothing in life is to be feared, it is only to be understood. Now is the time to understand more, so that we may fear less. — Marie Curie

Life can be mysterious if we use the wrong parameters to evaluate it. **First** and foremost, we cannot fully understand the whole by studying a small part. If we want to see the big picture, we must move away from one piece in isolation. We do not fully know a person if we only knew that person as a child. A human is all of its stages. Furthermore, we do not live just one life, but an everlasting series of lifetimes. Each lifetime is a mere spoke in an enormous wheel, a strand of fiber in an immense web, a mere page in a vast encyclopedia. Even though a segment does not fully reflect the deeper nature of life, it does give us hints and clues as to what that nature is. Hence, to evaluate our lives, we must take all of our many lives into consideration. More accurately, we must measure our lives using the yard stick of eternity. Knowing what it means to live temporal lives in a background of eternity allows us to better understand ourselves and evaluate our experiences.

Second, each life is like a play. It is enacted on a local stage, and for a definite purpose with a finite duration. Once one play is over, we exit and preparations are made for the next one. Just as there is a purpose for each play, there is a purpose for each life. We choose the purpose and we have the freedom to edit this choice at any moment. Everything is subject to change and we have the freedom to redirect our course. By merely making a better choice, we can alter our present and impact our future.

We are actors. Being eternal, we act in innumerable roles and under countless circumstances. We choose our role in each lifetime based on what is needed for the play to unfold so that its purpose is achieved – experiencing, learning life lessons and sculpting ourselves. We take the lead role in a few plays. In the majority of cases, however, we are in supporting roles, or even act as gofers in the background. At times, we are mere spectators as if on vacation. While spectators might judge an actor as brave, noble, a coward or a villain, the actors are not so. They are merely role-playing. This is why Christ taught us never to judge another.

> *Do not judge so that you will not be judged. For by the standard you judge you will be judged, and the measure you use will be the measure you receive.*   Matt 7:1-2

We could be playing agreed upon roles and not know it. Roles might be reversed next time around. We provide each other with opportunities to have the experiences needed.

Third, we must look at ourselves, not as weaklings trapped in a body with many limitations, but rather as souls occupying a body to have coveted physical experiences. With clear intentions and powerful tools such as visualization, contemplation and meditation, we can influence our genetics and shape our environments. We are always captains of our lives, never victims.

Fourth, a thorough understanding of dimensions is vital to comprehend the true nature of reality. It does not follow that life or reality are four dimensional just because we are four dimensional while in a physical body. We are multidimensional, functioning in the four dimensions for a specific period of time and for a unique view of reality. Once we understand the true meaning of dimensionality, we will have a much better understanding of the deeper nature of life and reality. We cannot realize our immortality because we are trapped in four dimensions. In this state, eternity and immortality are mere concepts that are detached from our reality.

Additionally, phenomena such as consciousness, mind and life are enigmas because we use four-dimensional logic to evaluate them. Birth and death are mysteries because we do not view them from the higher dimensions. Even though it is difficult to grasp higher dimensional realities, we are endowed with vision, imagination and fantasy to assist us.

Fifth, as we evolve, we begin to see more clearly and with fewer veils. Our understanding deepens and we know truths without intervening beliefs. Looking at life from the physical perspective, it appears flawed. Yet, viewing life from the higher dimensions, it is evident that life is perfect even with its apparent imperfections. Imperfections make life interesting, challenging and engaging. Without imperfections, life would lose its appeal.

Sixth, being immortal, we cannot always have "good and pleasurable" experiences. These, after a while, perhaps after a long while, become commonplace, monotonous, routine and boring. To make life livable, interesting and exciting, we must allow for the unpleasant and unexpected. These provide us the background so we may compare and contrast. Our experiences must be diverse. We must have opportunities to experience the vast range of feelings and emotions.

Seventh, Earth is a laboratory, a proving ground where we find out the limits of our endurance and capabilities. Some might discover how much pain and suffering they can endure. This teaches them not only about themselves, but also how to help others going through the same challenges. It also strengthens our empathy and compassion. While some might become acquainted with the incredible power of the human mind, others may discover the limits of their abilities. Still others might experience the ultimate sacrifice of love. There is no place like Earth for experimentation and discovery. We are in a physical laboratory, discovering, learning and sculpting ourselves.

MAKE THE MOST OF THIS LIFE

To make the most of this life, we must:

1. Learn how to live happy, healthy and productive lives
2. Master integration
3. Optimize living

1. Learn How to Live Happy, Healthy and Productive Lives

Because of Covid, I watched the 2020 summer Olympics in 2021. I was struck with the diversity of talented athletes and how fit each was for their specific skill. The winners in each category had the perfect mix of physical, emotional and mental qualities. Generally speaking, the sprinters had slender bodies with long strides. The discus throwers had large muscular arms, legs and chests. Basketball players were tall. Long distance runners were slender. Similarly, football players are specialized. Defensive players are bulky while the offense is agile. Looking at my body, I wondered what it was best suited for. This is when I realized that we cannot be anything we want, regardless of what we are told. I, for example, can never be a professional basketball player regardless of how well I train. I am simply too short.

Hence, the **first** criteria to live a happy, healthy and productive life is to discover what we are best suited for. What is the maximum use of our skills, talents, and abilities? How can we best use our physical, emotional and mental frameworks? These are our "talents". We must put these to best use given our conditions and circumstances. As Christ alluded in His parables, some start with a single talent, others five and a few ten. More than the number of talents, what is most important is what we do with what we have. We are a "package." How do we prepare this package for health, happiness and productivity? Some can be excellent carpenters, athletes, scientists, musicians or an endless variety of choices. **Our passions should lead the way.** Hence, we must discover what we are passionate about and excel at it.

Second, we must form habits that serve us. Habits automate and relegate to the subconscious what needs to be done. Excellent habits can keep us healthy, wealthy and wise. Detrimental habits can destroy us. Initially, we must consciously form a habit. Once ingrained, it executes automatically. Some excellent habits are positive mental attitude, efficiency, organization, promptness, responsibility and initiative.

2. Master Integration

We live on planet Earth. Earth is **one** planet. I live in the United States. The U.S. is **one** country, **one** nation.

I have **one** body. Even though Earth, the U.S. and my body are one, they are not a unit. The one is a multiplicity. Earth has people, animals, plants and minerals. The U.S. has people of diverse cultures and ethnicities. My body has systems, organs, tissues and cells. If these diversities coexist harmoniously and function as one, we have a mastermind group that can do and achieve any goal. If, however, these diversities act in their own selfish interests, then we have a house divided upon itself. It cannot stand for too long. There is nothing like multiplicity functioning in unity.

The discussion about the nature of God often centers on polytheism and monotheism. Which is it? It is both. God is a unity comprised of a multiplicity. In fact, the first verse in the Old Testament, *"In the beginning, God created the heavens and the earth. Gen 1:1"* has the word **Elohim** translated as a singular God when the word is plural, the gods. *In the beginning, **the gods** created the heavens and the earth.* That is why the question of whether God is one or many is mute. God is one and all. Some say that Hindus have 330 million gods which are of 33 types. In the Old Testament, God is referenced by 7 different names: **El, Elohim, Eloah, Elohai, El Shaddai, Jah, and Tzevaot.** Moslems have 99 traditional names for God that are epithets. Christians refer to God as a trinity of Father, Son and Holy Ghost. I adhere to the concept of E Pluribus Unum and E Unum Pluribus. All are correct. The one embodies the many.

Everything that exists is a different manifestation of the one reality. All are made of electrons, protons, neutrons and the same subatomic particles. Just because there are 99 names of God does not make God 99 different beings. Just because every item has a name does not change its ultimate nature. All of being is a unity manifesting a diversity. The important question is whether the multiplicity is functioning in unity or selfishly. Humans are unique in that we have freedom of choice. We can be as separate and independent, or as united and integrated as we choose to be.

When I was young, I remember my teacher demonstrating how working together as one was powerful. He held a pencil in his hand and easily broke it in two. He then collected all of our pencils and held them together. As hard as he tried to break them, he could not.

The human body is a perfect example of seamless integration – multiplicity functioning as a unit. It is a wonder to behold. Functioning as an integrated unit, we can move mountains. We can land on Mars. We can transform our Earth into a Heaven of our choosing.

There are three levels of integration:

    a. Intra-Integration (Personal)
    b. Inter-Integration (As a couple)
    c. Trans-Integration (As a group)

A. Intra-Integration (Personal)

There are two creation stories of humans in the Old Testament. In one version, The Lord creates humans as both male and female at the same time, just as He is.

> So God created man in his own image, in the image of God he created him; male and female he created them.   *Gen 1:27*

In the second version, He first creates the male and out of the male He creates the female.

> *So the LORD God caused a deep sleep to fall upon the man, and while he slept took one of his ribs and closed up its place with flesh. And the rib that the LORD God had taken from the man he made into a woman and brought her to the man.*   Gen 2:21-22

In the first story, humans are like God, both male and female at the same time. **This is the ideal state to be in – fully integrated.** In the second story, the male and the female are separate. They function as independent units – male and female. **This is our present reality**. It is our responsibility to bring these two aspects together, "wed" and integrate them so they are one as God intended for us to be. The symbolic meaning of the creation story is obvious. Each human being is both male and female at the same time. Each has masculine and feminine qualities. However, these have been separated and must be brought back together, integrated, "wedded" and made to function as one, as if they are one flesh.

It is interesting to note the symbolic meaning of the creation myth in Genesis. It states that God created everything in six days and then He rested. Five out of the six creations, He found to be **good**. "And God saw that it was good." (Gen 1:25) Not the last creation, though. For God saw that "It is **not** good for man to be alone." (Gen 2:18) So, out of man, He created woman. The symbolism of this story is obvious. Functioning alone is not good while intimate togetherness **is** fulfilling. In this story, Adam represents the male aspects while Eve is symbolic of the female and complementary aspects.

    We are both male and female. We have both Adam and Eve within us. To be happy, healthy and productive individuals, these must function seamlessly. They must be in an intimate embrace and a holy partnership. For it is **not good** for these to stand alone. They must become integrated as one. Some of our masculine qualities are reason, strength, decisiveness, justice, discipline, aggressiveness, and being an extrovert. Some of our feminine qualities are intuition, gentleness, compassion, empathy, tolerance, humility, softness, and being an introvert. The masculine qualities are directed by the brain while the feminine qualities are spearheaded by the heart. The Ancient Egyptian called these two the Ab and the Ba – mirror images of each other. In other words, they are complementary and must be used together. These two, the mind and the heart with their faculties, must be developed, perfected and "wedded" in each person.

    The individual is the main unit of the human species. We started life when the egg from our mother (feminine) and the sperm from our father (masculine) united in an embrace culminating in fertilization and the beginning of our life cycle. That is why we must integrate our masculine and feminine aspects to start our powerful developmental cycle. These two, the masculine and the feminine, must be acknowledged, harmonized and used together. They must be in constant partnership so that personal growth can be optimized. These complementary aspects must communicate, cooperate and integrate for optimum health, happiness and productivity.

An individual must start with a "self-integration" where he or she marries both of its aspects – the heart with the mind and intuition with reason. The male and female aspects must complement each other. The ancients termed this union, "The Alchemical Wedding of the King and Queen." An individual must learn to use any combination of its aspects the best way possible in any given situation. An individual must be able to reason and intuit, be strong and flexible, compassionate and just, loving and disciplinary. An individual who has attained self-integration of its complementary qualities is a well-adjusted individual who is able to do whatever is needed to be effective. Such an individual, both male and female, is then whole just as the original creation story intended for us to be.

B. Inter-Integration (As A Couple)

Once an individual is well-adjusted, or has "integrated" his or her complimentary qualities, that individual is ready for a "holy matrimony" with another. This is necessary, because there are qualities that we cannot develop on our own. We can cultivate discipline, reason and confidence, yet there are several important qualities that require an interaction with another to develop. These include mastering relationships, cooperation, love, caring, sharing, compassion, tolerance, and forgiveness, among others.

The next phase is for each male to find a female and for each female to find a male and partner with or "marry". This is an Alchemical marriage of the Sun and the Moon. Inter-marriage between two individuals makes the development of the higher emotions possible. When two hearts and two minds willingly unite in holy matrimony, the result can be beautiful and miraculous. The two individuals graduate from the school of individuality to that of the family. They begin to think and feel not only for themselves but equally for each other. If done properly, the quality of life will skyrocket for both. Their love will grow and blossom. Their personalities will become polished. Their circumstances will become more tolerable, enjoyable and abundance will prevail. Peace, contentment and joy will reign. Whereas communication, cooperation and partnering are evident in all species, humans can determine the degree of communication, cooperation and partnering between themselves. Marriage is the proving ground of this concept.

Marriage is the foundation of great achievements. That is why the first miracle of Christ was at a wedding – He turned water into wine. It takes a marriage to make a miracle happen. Marrying the "right" spouse makes all the difference in the quality of our lives. Just as it takes two hands to clap and make a noise, it is much easier to reach goals when two are working together. Partnering with my spouse, it was easier to purchase a house. Obviously, I could never have been able to have a family, know love and enjoy companionship had I been single.

We invented marriage because it provides innumerable benefits, if done right. Marriage is complicated and fraught with challenges; yet, the rewards are well worth it. Marriage is based on the desire of two humans to commune, cooperate and grow together. Intimacy is the ultimate desire for communion. Relationships are the means for mutual growth. Where one is lacking, the other provides. If cooperation is effective, quality of life soars.

The marriage of two individuals is not the annihilation of their individualities. It is not like sugar melting in water where both lose their identities. Marriage is the coming together of two where each contributes its strengths to compensate for the weaknesses of the other. Through marriage both can improve, continue to grow and excel. Even though individuality persists, the focus of each becomes the other. This is done willingly and gladly. Marriage is a breaking of the boundaries of the old self. It is integration, communion and partnering for mutual health, happiness and productivity.

In Genesis 2:24, it is stated:

Therefore, a man shall leave his father and his mother and hold fast to his wife, and they shall become one flesh.

A human being cannot feel whole until joined with a partner. We are not meant to be alone. We are social beings. Therefore, the best way to be healthy, happy and productive is to be in love with our life partner. Together, we can create, not only children, but also joy and abundance. Occasional strife is essential. It is part of life and it is a good stimulant for growth.

C. Trans-Integration (As A Group)

Communication, cooperation and mutual growth are the keys to success, happiness and abundance. They are not limited to two individuals, but should extend to all areas of life to form alliances, partnerships, companies, organizations and groups of like-minded individuals who come together to enhance the quality of their lives.

While intra-integration takes place in one individual and inter-integration takes place between two individuals, trans-integration spills over from two to three and beyond. Trans-integration starts when the married couple has children. With the birth of children, love and the sphere of selfhood extends from the married couple to include the offspring. Once the boundaries are broken to include "others", trans-integration can continue until it encompasses more and more groups. The family unit expands to include not only the children, but also relatives, friends, neighbors and even pets. Ultimately, the whole world can function as a unit.

Mutual growth should be the underlying reason for people to come together in the spirit of "one for all and all for one." There is no quicker way for humanity to advance than by working together. Breakthroughs will abound. Creativity will flourish and individuals will find it easier to express and fulfill their potentials. For an enlightening presentation on this subject, please read the chapter: "When two or more come together" in my book, **<u>Listening to the Voice Within, becoming enlightened</u>**.

For humanity to become integrated, it must first adopt a common language. This can happen if each country adopts two languages at a minimum – a common language that is taught by every nation and a local language. When humans communicate effortlessly and cooperate as one, anything is possible. They can partner on joint projects. They can say to the "mountain" move and the mountain will move. The intentional confusion of people so they cannot communicate and achieve greatness was a travesty. We must reverse it.

> Now the whole earth had one language and the same words. And as people migrated from the east, they found a plain in the land of Shinar and settled there. And they said to one another, "Come, let us make bricks, and burn them thoroughly." And they had brick for stone, and bitumen for mortar. Then they said, "Come, let us build ourselves a city and a tower with its top in the heavens, and let us make a name for ourselves, lest we be dispersed over the face of the whole earth." And the LORD came down to see the city and the tower, which the children of man had built. And the LORD said, "Behold, they are one people, and they have all one language, and this is only the beginning of what they will do. And nothing that they propose to do will now be impossible for them. Come, let us go down and there confuse their language, so that they may not understand one another's speech." So the LORD dispersed them from there over the face of all the earth, and they left off building the city. Therefore its name was called Babel, because there the LORD confused the language of all the earth. And from there the LORD dispersed them over the face of all the earth.
>
> *Gen 11:1-9*

3. Optimize Living

What is the most effective way to live? What is the best course of action in each lifetime? Simply, it is to utilize the opportunities we are presented with, or that we can create, to demonstrate excellence, to be of service, to develop a skill, to enhance an ability or add to our toolbox of experiential knowledge.

We live to sculpt ourselves into works of art. As we improve, so does the world since we are an integral part of the world. Our "life-work" begins with ourselves. Just as a baby grows slowly and wholly, so it is with us. We must grow emotionally, mentally, and spiritually. We must continue to improve our relationships and expand our love and appreciation for ourselves and others. We must cultivate the qualities that we lack. We are apprentices in the process of becoming masters of our circumstances. Since each person is at a different stage in their life's journey, each has its own issues to work on. These issues are more evident than we realize, often staring us in the face – our weaknesses appearing as challenges. Yet, we seldom see them as opportunities to face with determination and courage.

Some need to work on being decisive. Others might need to cultivate forgiveness, tolerance or acceptance. Our circumstances are the mirror that reflects back to us the nature of the lessons we need to learn and the actions we should take. "Veils" block our view and "scales" in our eyes prevent us from seeing clearly. These "veils" and "scales" are inflated egos, ignorance, prejudice, judgement, greed and many other vices. We need to work on our weaknesses (vices) and transform them into strengths (virtues).

Where we currently are in our lives is an indication of what we have been able to achieve so far and is the springboard to where we decide to go next. At any juncture in our lives, we have the option to change course. We always have freedom of choice. We are the captains of our "ships". We hold the keys to our destiny. We can move forward or stagnate in place.

Looking at the lives of family members, relatives, friends and acquaintances, we realize the vast diversity of life styles. People's interests and the choices they make vary greatly. They have different careers and their health, wealth and circumstances are diverse.

Why do people make different choices under similar situations? Family members undergoing the same experiences react differently resulting in vastly different outcomes. Why?

Our interests vary in sports, entertainment, food, clothing, education, careers, and life styles. Are these differences due merely to brain chemistry or is there a deeper reason?

It takes everyone to make the human experience what it is. This love of diversity is innate in humans because we are immortals. We have lived before and will live again and again and, in each lifetime, we try out new interests. Having experienced something before, we might try something new or we might try the same thing again because we remember that we enjoyed it before.

Similarly, if we tried something in a past life and did not find it interesting, we will try to avoid it this time around. Memory is not only conscious; it is often subconscious and at times instinctual. Our personalities are the result of eons of accumulated experiences and their memories. We carry our past within us in our genes as skills, talents and proclivities. Our personalities are the archives of our past life history.

We determine the quality of our lives. To make the most out of this lifetime, we must evaluate some of our important choices. Would we choose privacy or fame? Wealth or sufficiency? Would we choose that people think highly of us even at the expense of our integrity or would we choose to be who we are regardless of what others think? Would we solely pursue entertainment and personal pleasure or would we emphasize the building of our character and the polishing of our personality? Would we choose selfishness or would we display generosity and altruism? How would you choose to live?

A. Privacy Or Fame

What are we aiming for, privacy or fame? Is it more important to be famous at the expense of privacy? Obviously, there are many who would love to be famous and give up their privacy. Yet there are many who are famous and bemoan the loss of their privacy. They would gladly give up their fame for the enjoyment of anonymity. Neither privacy nor fame in and of themselves are good or bad. It is wise, however, before seeking fame to know the price one has to pay. If, after evaluation, one is ready to bear the consequences, then go for it by all means. Since the consequences of some actions are irreversible, we must carefully evaluate our actions before undertaking them.

So, what would it be for you? Would you rather live a private life or be famous with little privacy? Would you rather come and go as you please, or would you rather have paparazzi chasing you wherever you go? Do you want to be left alone to enjoy your simple and private life or do you prefer the publicity that goes with fame? Or do you prefer somewhere in between?

B. Wealth Or Sufficiency

Wealth is great if it is used to enhance the quality of life of the individual and others. Wealth can get in the way of spiritual growth if it is the object of our pursuit. It is wonderful to have enough to cover our needs and wants. Yet, we should examine our lives carefully. Too many wants can distract us from what is really important. Many accumulate wealth for status and prestige. That is their choice and there is no judgement against them. This decision, however, must be carefully evaluated. Not everyone can handle wealth. There are several instances where sudden wealth destroyed lives. There are those who won large sums of money, yet ended up poor after only a few years. Since we cannot take wealth with us, accumulating money makes no sense unless there is a plan for using it. It is far better to spread the wealth and share it to bring joy to others than to simply hoard and store it. Wealth avails us the opportunity to touch the lives of others. We must decide between greed and true wealth. While greed accumulates, hoards and keeps, true wealth empowers, ennobles and enriches lives.

We can be wealthy without owning much. We are fortunate to live in a country with many state and national parks. They are treasures to appreciate and enjoy. We do not have to labor or maintain them. Visit and take advantage of these precious gems. With a meager entrance fee, we can walk in as owners, for we are. Take care of them and preserve them for posterity. It is our children's inheritance.

C. Time Well Spent Vs. Time Wasted

We start each day with 24 hours to do with as we please. What we do with these precious hours is what sets us apart. Some waste time, others kill time, while wise ones use it productively. Time is currency we can trade to acquire skills and abilities. It is alright to waste some time, but the majority of our time should be used wisely.

We should consider allocating our time. After taking care of necessities like work and chores, we can spend time for what we value and enjoy. We can share time with loved ones, bonding and enhancing relations. We should have time for rest, play and relaxation. We should also allocate time to enjoy privately. Having time for oneself to be alone or in nature to think, to plan and to reflect can be rejuvenating. It is also worthwhile to allocate time for education and self-improvement. Reading, studying and enjoying the arts can make a vast difference in the quality of our lives.

When asked what they regret most, some wealthy and famous individuals replied that they wished they had spent more time with loved ones. Accumulating money or more possessions was seldom one of their regrets.

D. Health And Disease

Staying healthy is important. It is our responsibility to take care of our health. Doctors can help us but we are the primary providers for the welfare of our bodies. We are the caretakers of not only our bodies, but also of our emotions and minds. We must learn to live preventive lives. This is not as difficult as it seems. Moderation in life style, a nutritious diet, rest, play and staying active go a long way in keeping us healthy and fit. We can learn how to maintain our health, vigor, and vitality.

It is our choice whether we eat to live or live to eat. Enjoyment of food is important, but not at the expense of our health. Desserts taste great, but too much dessert can lead to innumerable health problems. Following our appetites have their consequences and these might not be what we want for a quality life. Do we eat for health and vigor or do we eat to fill our bellies? Do we choose taste or do we choose nutritional value? Do we eat just enough or do we overeat? Do we eat because we are hungry or do we eat out of habit? Do we eat alone or share our meal with loved ones?

How about drinks? There is nothing wrong with alcoholic beverages if they are regulated. Addictions, however, can be devastating. We must consider our actions before an addiction takes hold. It is easy to nip a bad habit in the bud. It is easy to pluck a tiny weed than to wait for it to become a mighty tree. We should only form habits that serve us.

It is sad to see young people smoking. Where is the intelligence in that? Yet, many undertake smoking without any consideration of the consequences. It is natural to try things and to experiment, but it is not OK to continue abusing our bodies once the dangers are known and the consequences are evident.

E. Living For A Day Vs. Living For A Lifetime

We do not live for today only. We are here to live a lifetime. Granted, we do not know when we might die, but that does not mean not to plan for tomorrow. We can live the best we know how today while we plan for a long and healthy life. We do not have to sacrifice everything for tomorrow, yet some sacrifice today for a better tomorrow is wise indeed. That is why we educate ourselves. Education lays the foundation for a better tomorrow. Investing in ourselves is wise. We can sacrifice some of our play time for self-improvement. We can save some of our money for a rainy day. These are not foolish acts even if we die tomorrow.

Living is like driving a car. We must not only be aware of the cars in our immediate surroundings, we must also scan ahead and look back. Scanning forward and looking back gives us not only a better perspective but it also makes our ride smoother. By examining our past, we can learn from our mistakes and by planning for our future, we can prepare not only for rainy days, but more importantly for a better retirement and a richer old age.

We can learn to derive pleasure from what currently requires effort. All it takes is a change in attitude. How we view a task makes a big difference. We can learn to enjoy necessary tasks that we do not care for by pretending that they are "fun" or "relaxing" until they become so. What we consider pleasurable can be learned. Undertaking difficult but important tasks can be a source of pride. We can enjoy saving. Seeing our accumulated savings grow can make it possible for us to plan a much-desired vacation.

There are gradations to pleasure. Some pleasures are fleeting while others are enduring. Physical pleasures are temporary and their effects fade with time. Mental and spiritual pleasures derived from continuous growth and learning are ongoing. They endure. We can pursue and enjoy them throughout our lives.

Our academic education begins when we enter school. We progress through kindergarten, elementary and secondary schools. If we are fortunate, we go to college and progress from being a freshman, sophomore, and junior to being a senior and graduating. Education does not end once we finish school. It is a never-ending pursuit. Extra-curricular activities, interests, hobbies and passions are doorways that can lead us to avocations, contentment and peace of mind. Even though our physical growth comes to an end, mental, emotional and spiritual growth do not have to. We can continue to learn and improve.

F. Quality Vs. Quantity

Another consideration is quality vs. quantity. Do we want to have many acquaintances or just have a few quality friends? Do we want lots and lots of shoes, pots and pans, or do we want just a few good ones? Once more, either way is fine. However, being aware of our choices is important. We can be trapped into accumulating and hoarding beyond our needs which becomes a burden for us or our loved ones once we depart.

Even more important than having many or a few quality items is having the right items. Often, we do not plan on what we really want and end up with having "things". Being selective in what we want is a primary virtue. One of our most irresponsible acts is the nonchalant attitude toward having children. For many, this is done without planning. It is often accidental. Yet, doing a good job of raising a child is one of the most important responsibilities we can undertake. It requires planning, foresight and sacrifice. Many poor and uneducated people have no recourse to birth control. They simply have children as a natural consequence of intercourse. My father typified this way of life. His motto was: "I have the children and God will take care of them." Why not limit the number of our children to those we can actually care for and provide for all their needs, especially a quality environment, education, time and love?

Even more important is knowing value by pursuing what is essential. While many chase treasures of the world, a few seek a far superior treasure buried within. This treasure within is in the form of a seed. It must be cared for and cultivated before it can grow and manifest its transformative capabilities. This seed is our "talent" buried within. It is our soul. For Christians, it is the Kingdom of God within. For Moslems, it is the will of God. In fact, the word Islam means allowing the will of God to function through us. To be a true Moslem is to give up one's will and live to do the will of God. Doing the will of God does not mean abandoning reason and logic. It does not imply reading books whether holy or not and unquestioningly following their dictates. It does not mean accepting interpretations by so called experts. It simply means being true to our higher selves and always listening to The Voice Within. We can read books and listen to others all we want, but we must **always** refer to our inner guide as to what we accept as true and how we live our lives. It is our responsibility to live our lives as well as we know how to. Integrity is being true to our self. We must follow the dictates of our conscience and live to express our values and ideals. We must be at peace with who we are and what we stand for.

G. Drama Vs. Peace

Some get used to drama in their lives and feel the need for it. Creating drama is a choice. Arguing and quarrelling with others is also a choice. Some get so used to stress that it becomes their normal way of life. We must decide what is important. Which do we prefer, being right or being at peace? To win an argument or to give in and avoid the drama? Are we willing to sacrifice pride for peace and tranquility? Many of our difficulties are self-created and our wounds are self-inflicted. It is our choice to be happy or to complain and be miserable. Some demand a lot before they are happy, yet it requires very little to make them miserable. Is this intelligent? Why not reverse the process? Why not become adept at minimizing stress and maximizing gratification? It is far more important to give in to trivial arguments and be happy than to try to prove that we are right. Being compassionate, understanding and sympathetic is healing. Proving that we are superior could be due to lack of self-esteem. We must choose our actions carefully. Every action has consequences. It is wise to choose health over stress, happiness over misery, people's feelings over pride.

H. Solitude Vs. Fellowship

One of the most important skills we can cultivate is mastering relationships. The measure of success for our lives is the ability to relate to people regardless of who they are. If we can relate to the humanness of others, regardless of their veneer, then we are doing well. Valuing and appreciating the uniqueness and individuality of others are sure signs of maturity. Nurturing deep and abiding relations is at the heart of why we choose to be born. We can derive the utmost joy from the few but intimate associations we cultivate.

Some do far better when relating to a small group than to a multitude. Others prefer the company of many. Even though it is great being with others, it is vital to have some time for solitude. Solitude is an elixir that can rejuvenate. Being alone in nature recharges us. Solitude helps us to see and think clearly. When with people, we listen to others. In solitude, we listen to nature and The Voice Within.

I. Belief Vs. Knowledge

Why do we have unexamined beliefs? What makes us hold on and defend detrimental teachings? It is easy to understand that we do this as children. Once we grow up, however, we must examine what we believe and let go of beliefs that are simply untrue or do not help us live healthy, happy and productive lives.

We are brought up to believe and follow rather than to think and question. Many of our beliefs come from religion and politics. Early humans attributed natural phenomena to gods. They had gods of thunder, lightning, volcanos and hurricanes. This is understandable for they had no real knowledge of the causes. But why attribute these natural events to gods? Animals hear thunder, see lightning and experience earthquakes, hurricanes and volcanoes. Yet, they do not have a need to create gods for these phenomena. Why us? Is it because we fear and feel helpless? Is it ignorance?

Believing we can appease the gods, religion created ceremonies, rituals and sacrifice. Being social, yearning to make sense of our environment and to belong, we accept these traditions without question. Since we do not have a better explanation, we accept what religion has to offer. Yet, with some effort, knowledge is available.

We are emotional beings. It is easy to prey on us by appealing to our emotions. The stock market relies on greed and fear. Religion and politics rely on our need to belong and be accepted. Followers are always welcomed. Independent thinkers and questioners are shunned. For religion, we are sheep in need of a shepherd. We are clay in the hands of the potter. We can be molded and shaped into whatever they desire.

This cannot be the story of our lives. We can work with any group for the common good. Yet, we do not have to believe and accept teachings that only encourage following without questioning. We are individuals. We have minds to think, hearts to feel and intuition to know. We have a voice within that shows us the way. We have nothing to fear, not even death for we will live again. So why not examine our beliefs? Substitute knowledge where available and always keep an open mind. Questioning is healthy and necessary. We are aspects of the divine, not sheep or clay.

C. PLAN OUR NEXT LIFE

Before we plan our next life, we must reflect on this one. What are some of the important lessons we learned? What are some of our regrets? What are some of our memorable triumphs? Reflecting on lessons learned is critical for improving our chances for a better next life. Here are a few of my most valuable lessons:

1. People are important, not self-gratification. Taking advantage of another for any gain is selfish, childish and immature. Forgoing temporary pleasures and demonstrating generosity instead has a more lasting impact. Relationships, based on trust and appreciation, can endure and be the source of comradery, satisfaction, comfort and joy.
2. Always doing the important things **first**. Learning to discard a mountain of trivia and pursuing the critical few instead. This is the 80/20 rule. 80% of all we undertake is trivia. Selecting and pursuing the critical few is wise indeed. Spending time with family, cultivating abiding friendships and taking good care of ourselves are among the critical few.
3. Cultivating our minds through education is vital. It made a difference in the quality of my life. Continuous education of diverse subjects, and command of the native language are of the

utmost importance.
4. Establishing habits that serve instead of ones that detract from our well-being. We must examine our habits, nurturing the beneficial ones and replacing the harmful ones. Additionally, we should examine our thoughts, attitudes and beliefs, feeding the constructive and weeding out the destructive.
5. Going for sufficiency of wants and needs and avoiding the trap of greed. Knowing value and setting boundaries are important.
6. Living a simple, unencumbered life.
7. Always doing our best in any role we find ourselves in – employer or employee, student or teacher, friend, father or mother, husband or wife. Doing our best is a reflection of our character.

Make a short list of the successes you are proud of and dwell on them. Perhaps you would like to repeat such successes in your next life.

Make another short list of your regrets and dwell on them. Perhaps you can avoid making similar mistakes in your next life.

Our actions generate reactions. These are the consequences that manifest as karma. Karmic forces automatically attract us to the circumstances we need to encounter and resolve. We can eliminate most of our future bad karma by preventing their causes in the first place. We can greatly influence the type of life we will have in our next life if we become aware now and consciously plan what we value.

The decision of how to live our lives can be made on either side of the veil. Even though the blueprint, planning and the groundwork are laid out while we are on the other side, the actual implementation takes place while we are physical. We can change course anytime by exercising our freedom of choice. Since we have the power to plan our life, what would we choose for our next life? Would we pick an impactful life or the life of a commoner? Would we select power and influence or would we rather be an ordinary person?

Let us imagine that we are in "The Assembly" with the elders. We can submit any request for a future life. What kind of life would we choose? The more we know what we want and why we want it, the easier it is for us to experience it in our next life. Knowing what we want is akin to creating the seeds that when released, will scatter in the wind and settle in the "ether." These seeds will establish roots, begin to grow, and will attract to themselves that which is in accordance to their nature. It is for us to create the seeds and release them. The cosmic takes care of the actualization. Here are some items to consider:

A. Physical Attributes

Physical attributes are an important consideration. Should we have a perfect body? Should we have a physical challenge so that we can overcome it and grow? Do we want to be born as a minority race or be part of the majority? Each has its benefits and its challenges. Do we want to be tall, medium or short? What type of parents should we choose? Should we select poor parents who love us or rich parents who give us a lot of material goods but might neglect us? We can even pick parents who make our lives difficult and give us the opportunity to overcome, grow and triumph. Do we want to be healthy or sickly? Once more each condition has its benefits and its challenges. Obviously, with each life cycle, we can choose based on what we have already experienced. We should welcome experiences that help us grow and mature.

Here are my choices:

I would rather be born into a poor family. I prefer to create my abundance than be born into it. Furthermore, being poor, I would appreciate abundance once I have it. I would also be able to relate to the poor who are the vast majority of the people of the planet. I would much rather be poor early on in life than in my old age. If I am to suffer, I would rather do it early on. Being poor can also teach us value. Experiencing lack allows us to appreciate having, once the circumstances change.

I would not choose to have a perfect body. I would rather be challenged in some way. Having a perfect body might attract many unwanted suitors. Being challenged in some way would only attract those who can see through the handicap and it would place relationships on a more solid foundation. Not being perfect is a great motivator to improve and excel.

Of more importance than a perfect physical body is having a sharp mind. Being intelligent is far more advantageous than physical beauty. Our minds are our greatest assets. A keen mind makes all the difference in the quality of our lives and whether or not we succeed. Being intelligent, we can live creative lives and contribute to society.

B. Choosing Our Spouse

The choice of a spouse can make or break a person. Choose the right spouse and you will be blessed and abide in heaven. Choose the wrong spouse and you will be in hell. How can we make the right choice? What should we look for? Is it looks? Is it attraction? Or is it in the kiss as the song states?

If we keep our eyes open, we can avoid setbacks later on. From the beginning, there are always indications as to how things will pan out. We are not as blind of the future as we assume ourselves to be unless we choose to close our eyes and not see.

Being attentive and observant, analyzing, reflecting, meditating, praying and asking for guidance are sure ways of making a wise choice. The chemistries of the two must match and be compatible. Above all, kissing must be enjoyable. We must find the other physically attractive, desirable to touch and be with. The spouse should be emotionally enriching, mentally stimulating and spiritually compatible and uplifting. Above all, a spouse is a partner.

Obviously, finding the perfect life partner is not easy. In fact, it is very challenging. If we make the right choice, we are fortunate indeed. We should be sympathetic toward those who find themselves with the "wrong" spouse. How we attract and find our life partner varies. Yet, once we locate the "right" partner, we will know it. I certainly did.

Who is the "right" partner?

Someone with whom we can build and enjoy a life together. Someone who complements our traits. Where we are weak, our partner is strong. Where our partner is weak, we are strong. If we both love to shop and continuously spend, then we will probably face financial difficulties. If we can plan and execute our goals together, we will have a greater chance of success.

Our spouse is also someone who will expose us to our weaknesses and even throw some challenges in our path. This is normal for we need to grow. Fortunately, life never dishes out more than we can handle. We are born to face some challenges and hopefully, overcome them and gain mastery. In the process, we cultivate our character and develop our personality.

C. Relationships

We learn the most from our interactions with others. How we relate to others is a measure of our communication skills. If we master this art, we can be happy. However, relationships are not easy to master. Nothing worthwhile is. Yet, mastering this skill is vital to our success and happiness. How do we excel in our relationships? We must be excellent **listeners** and communicators. We often need to go through difficulties, misunderstandings, disagreements, quarrels, and heartaches before we finally master the art of relating to others.

Remembering that each person is in their own world with unique perspectives, opinions and experiences helps us relate better. Some believe that compromise is the answer. I believe in the 80/20 rule. Eighty percent of all that we encounter is irrelevant, trivial and not worth fighting over. We must learn to discern what is important. Matters of principle are important, yet even these should take a back seat when it comes to hurting another's feelings unnecessarily. Peace and harmony are more important than ego and being right. We compromise when we can. Yet, in important matters, we must stand our ground. We cannot help another realize a mistake, learn and grow if we constantly give in or compromise.

I learned many of my life lessons from my immediate family. I learned invaluable lessons from my wife and daughters. I am eternally indebted to them for the lessons they taught me about how to better relate to them and others. None of these would be possible if we do not listen and are not willing to change. **Listening and willingness to improve are the key.**

D. Circumstance

As we live, we cultivate unique skills and abilities and build our toolset. Confidence is one of the most important tools we can have. To build our confidence, we must successfully face and overcome challenges. Our confidence grows, one encounter at a time, the more we face difficulties and overcome them.

Therefore, I would not choose an easy life. Difficulty has its advantages. Challenges have an important place in our lives. They are the exercises we need to develop our "muscles." I would, however, choose to face my challenges early on. I would rather live my difficult years while young than when I am in my later years. I would rather enjoy an easier old age. When young, it is acceptable to face challenges and encounter difficulties. Old age should be for reaping the benefits from our earlier more challenging life. During old age, we should focus on family, hobbies, travelling and appreciating our beautiful planet and its wonderful inhabitants.

I would also plan a diverse life. I would not want to be born, live and die in the same vicinity. Earth is a magical planet and we should roam about and settle in an area that feels right for us. Following our inner feelings, we can choose where to live. From this home base, we can explore the rest of the planet as time and resources permit.

I would want to meet and cultivate friendships with a diverse group of people from many nationalities, backgrounds, races and religions. I would also undertake excursions to experience diverse cultures to become a well-rounded mature individual. I would learn about the various sciences, arts, religions and philosophies. I would study ancient and modern spiritual teachings and contribute to society by sharing what I learn. I would want to be a thinker, influencer and a unique individual.

E. Skill Set

How would you like to earn your living next time around? Most people are specialized. They are either mental or mechanical, in the arts or the sciences. Would you like to be a great musician? A sculptor? A painter? Perhaps a scientist? Would you like to excel at some sport? If you decide on what you would like to experience next time and you meditate on it, you can make it happen. It would be fascinating to try something totally different from what you are doing this lifetime. To excel might require us to devote our entire life to developing and mastering a desired skill. This is easier if based on a passion. Since it helps to start training while young, it is a privilege to be born again and start fresh with the right circumstances.

F. Place Of Birth

Would you like to be born in an affluent country? Or, would you rather learn what it feels like to be born in a country with far less opportunities? Regardless of where you choose to be born, remember that you can move around. Your country of birth does not have to be the country of your permanent residence. It is good to live under a variety of circumstances and learn through them. It helps us mature quickly.

G. Sex

What sex would you like to be born as next time? Male? Female? How about the opposite sex of what you are now? It would be wonderful to learn from experience what it is like to be the other sex. Quite often, we do not appreciate the other sex enough, but if we lived as one, then we would know, understand and truly value the opposite sex.

Your next life is in your hands. Plan it well.

PART VI

Final Thoughts

THE HUMAN EXPERIENCE REVISITED

There's no glory in climbing a mountain if all you want to do is to get to the top. It's experiencing the climb itself - in all its moments of revelation, heartbreak, and fatigue - that has to be the goal.   *– Karyn Kusama*

We are no longer surrounded by mysteries. We are born. We know where we came from – the other side of the veil, the spiritual realm. We die. We know what happens – we enter a state similar to the dream world. We have religions because we know for sure that there is a God. This God is LOVE, BEAUTY and JOY. There is no judgement. Free will is unconditional. We are led to believe that some mysteries are beyond human comprehension. This is not true. We can understand. We can know. Everything makes perfect sense with cyclic immortality. We now understand the nature of life. We struggle, suffer, age and die because we are immortal. We require endless varieties of experiences. We not only struggle, suffer, age and die, we also experience joy, intimacy, laughter, wonder, beauty and love. Now we know for certain that we do not have a soul, we are soul. We also have a better understanding of the role and nature of evil. This gives us the opportunity to stand up to evil, learn its causes, transform it and prevent it from happening in the future.

Having answers definitely makes a difference.

We are not merely evolved beasts. There is another aspect to us. Just as the Old Testament states, we have an animal part. (*Ecclesiastes 3:18-22*.) It is our body with its operating system of passions and survival instinct. These die with the body. Yet, we have a more important aspect that unequivocally sets us apart from animals. It is our soul with its advanced "software" of compassion, love, creativity and appreciation of the sublime. This is why there is an important distinction between us and our closest animal relatives, the apes and chimpanzees. While they have 24 pairs of chromosomes, we have 23. The fusion of two small pairs of chromosomes in humans to form a single chromosome was no accident. It was directed by consciousness to set us apart as distinct and unique beings capable of learning, growing and maturing.

We evolved to be what we are because evolution is directed toward ever-increasing diversity, efficiency, miniaturization, higher consciousness and better collaboration. We are on the verge of directing the course of our own evolution through conscious intent and freedom of choice. Consciousness is at the helm directing our advancement.

The "need" for diversification is an overarching "intent" in nature. That is why inbreeding is frowned upon and discouraged, even in animals. In fact, the main reason sex evolved is to ensure diversification. While the vast majority of cells are content to reproduce asexually maintaining their "purity", only egg and sperm cells divide sexually. Sex cells have single strand chromosomes. They not only cross over, but unite with chromosomes from the other parent, thus, ensuring diversity. Diversity is important to life because it allows us to form mastermind groups, thus, accelerating the pace of our growth and maturation.

To better understand the nature of the human experience, let us revisit a few facts we considered at the beginning:

- We are born with an expiration date – we live, we age and we die. We have differing life spans. Some live until old age while others die young.

- *This is fair because lifespan is based on purpose. Those who live until old age have a time-consuming purpose. They live until they finish their life's mission. The ones who die young have a purpose that can be achieved quickly. They will be reborn fresh and ready for another purpose that might require them to live longer lives. Additionally, those who die young give their parents and society an opportunity to learn important lessons, change views, or advocate for needed changes.*

- Each individual has gifts and challenges. While some are intellectuals, others are endowed with natural proclivities. Living affords us a diversity of experiences ranging from painful to pleasurable, from struggle to comfort, from defeat to triumph, from agony to joy. Many live in abject poverty while a few live in luxurious abundance.

- *This is not by chance. Life is fair. It is not governed by "luck of the draw". Everyone starts with the original one "talent". We are expected to invest our talent and in each lifetime double what we started with. Because of freedom of choice, some invest wisely while others do not. We determine the nature of our experiences. It is up to us how many "talents" we end up with based on how industrious we have been. Additionally, we take turns playing the different roles. One lifetime we might be poor, but can be wealthy next time around.*

- Our memory is selective and fragmented. Even after our nervous system is fully developed, we instinctively dismiss and forget what is not important. A filter is always in place. We retain only the highlights of our lives. How does the brain decide what is important for us? Is survival the only criteria?
- *For the brain, survival is the only criteria. For the soul, it is growth and maturation through a variety of experiences.*

- Our understanding is ever increasing. Each generation builds on the achievements of the previous one. As we experience, learn and grow, we progress toward maturity. We have come a long way. Yet, we remain barbaric in many ways. We are extremely efficient killing machines. Why? Why do we still have wars after millions of years of evolution?
- *Wars are a reflection of the stage humanity is currently in. We started as infants, went through childhood, advanced through adolescence and are now poised to approach adulthood and maturity. When we do, wars will be considered barbaric. We will cooperate more and we will have peace on Earth.*

- Even though our bodies are constantly changing, we are always aware of ourselves as unique, individual entities. This awareness is constant, ever present, and rides the waves of change and impermanence. How and why do we maintain our sense of identity?
- **Our soul is our identity. While our basic soul never changes, our epi-soul does. We are constantly adding to our epi-soul which grows and blossoms with our experiences. Basic soul is who we are. Epi-soul is who we are becoming.**
- We are a link in a vast chain, a thread in the enormous web of life. Yet, we are seldom aware of this. We live as if we are separate entities. Even though we refer to ourselves as individuals, in reality, there is no such thing. We do not have a separate existence. We require food, water and air to survive. These are separate from us. Our bodies exist because of planet Earth. We are utterly dependent on all else for our survival. Therefore, true individuality as an independent entity is an illusion. We are a process rather than a finished product. We are nothing more than a link in the chain, a thread in the web, or a cell in the body linking all. Is our purpose merely to propagate our species? Why aren't we more aware of our interconnectedness? If we were, would we cooperate more and kill less?
- *Physically, we do not have a separate individuality. Spiritually, however, each has a unique identity as a unique expression of divinity. As we grow and mature, we will wake up and realize our interconnectedness. We will stop killing and cooperate more.*

- Since the body is subject to disease, aging and death, evolution of the physical body cannot be the ultimate purpose of nature. Our physical bodies are not at the top of physical evolution. It is evident that many of us depend on medications to make it through old age. Examining our physical faculties, we notice that we have given up many of our physical acuities as we evolved intellectually. Animals are far better when it comes to physical prowess and the senses. Our sense of hearing and smell are worse than even some of our pets; our vision is pathetic compared to many other species. Why have we stopped improving many of our faculties? If we are at the top of the evolutionary scale, how come our faculties are not? Is mental evolution all that matters? Why can't we be the best mentally and physically?
- *Physical faculties are aspects of our spirit and the operating system of the body. They are for our survival. Additionally, if our physical faculties were perfect, we might miss out on some important experiences such as pain and handicaps. We are not on Earth to have perfect bodies, but rather to experience the sublime, develop our minds, build our character and personality, and cultivate the noble emotions of love, sympathy, empathy and compassion.*

- Our mental, social, and spiritual evolution are indeed highly advanced. It is clear that mentally, we are advancing; spiritually, we are maturing; and socially, we are progressing. These are what set us apart and distinguish us from other species. Are these what matter most?

- *Yes. What matters most is developing our epi-souls. Hence cultivating the higher emotions and mastering visualization, imagination and creativity are vital.*

- We do not live to merely survive even though survival is essential. Quality of life matters. We pursue value and meaning. We endeavor to know and understand. We get bored with mere existence. We seek newness, adventure, excitement, and thrill. Even though we continue to display the primitive emotions of anger, hate, prejudice and superiority, it is apparent that we are evolving the higher emotions of empathy, forgiveness, acceptance, love, compassion, and inclusiveness. Are these the trend of our evolution?

- *Yes. The body and its functions evolve naturally. We are on Earth to grow our epi-soul and its attributes.*

- We are social beings. Even though we can survive on our own, we urgently seek others. We require contact and intimacy. We crave touch and connection. Sex plays a major role in our lives because we have an urge to commune, be intimate, and perpetuate life. This is ingrained in us and beyond our control. By having children, we connect the past with the future. We enable the advancement of the species. More importantly, we afford an opportunity for others to be born, live, experience, age and die just as we had these opportunities. Is this all there is to life?

- *Experiencing wonder, waking up to beauty, becoming compassionate and developing our character and personality are the main reasons for living. These are aspects of the epi-soul.*

- We remain oblivious to the deeper meaning of many of our experiences. We have no clue as to what an out-of-body experience really is. Many have near-death experiences. We do not know what these are. A few have experienced extra-sensory perception, yet we have no clue what it is. Even dreams baffle us. We pray, but how many of us know for sure who we are praying to, and if our prayers are received and processed?
- *Our Higher Self "hears" our prayers and responds. We are shown what we can do. It is up to us to act. Our higher faculties are the fruit of our developing epi-souls. When we pray, we should only seek guidance on what our next steps should be.*
- We are confined to our limited world. We seldom venture beyond our comfort zone. We view the world through the aperture of a personal camera focused on what we consider to be important at the time. Yet, if we move the camera around, or better yet, if we pull away from the camera altogether, we see an entirely different vista.
- *Practicing detachment and rising above the trivial and mundane is the "adult" way to live.*
- We are blessed beyond measure. Yet, we seldom stop complaining. Being alive is reason enough to rejoice. If we are advanced in age, we should celebrate, for many have died young. Some complain that they are single, unmarried, yet forget that not all married couples are happy. Some who are married complain that they have no children, yet forget that every child is a blessing to its parents, but

not necessarily to society. There are many criminals out there; they were children once. Instead of focusing on what we lack, we should appreciate what is at hand. Perhaps we will stop complaining about lacking shoes when we meet someone lacking feet or legs, as the saying goes.

- *Practicing gratitude, appreciating our gifts and enjoying the blessings conferred on us is wise indeed. There is a lot to be thankful for if we open our eyes, minds and hearts.*

- I, like many, have been inspired on many occasions. Yet, who knows where inspiration comes from? Why do songs, music, the arts and beauty touch our souls? Why do our spirits soar when we are in love?

- *We are touched and we soar because we are endowed with soul. The more evolved our epi-soul, the more we appreciate the sublime.*

- How do we explain prodigies?
- *They have lived before and are able to tap into previously developed talents and abilities.*

- How can we reconcile the belief in God with accidents and natural disasters that cause the death of thousands of innocent people? How can we explain incredible human atrocities such as genocides?
- *Nature is evolving. Disasters are not always "bad." They harbor the seeds of renewal. If we view life through the lens of eternity, then all is well. Even those who perish come back and are born again. Human atrocities are perpetrated by humans with immature epi-souls. We are the agents of change. We*

have a role to play. It is up to us to make a difference.

Faced with the vastness of being, a plethora of destructive natural forces and an abundance of mysteries, it is easy to feel insignificant. This is one view. Alone, we are weak indeed. No individual needs to be alone unless they choose to. As part of the whole, we are powerful, capable and resourceful. We stand on the shoulders of those who preceded us. We, in turn, can be the shoulders for those who will follow us. Together, we can solve our problems, unveil the mysteries, and live abundantly.

I learned a great deal from others. Now I am giving back. It is my hope to contribute to those who want to benefit from my experiences. I was enabled. It is time to empower others. There is no limit to how much we can learn and do together. The solution to the riddles and mysteries of life has been revealed. Let us make the most of **the greatest revelation ever. Let us incorporate these findings into our lives.**

CONCLUSION

The idea for this book is based on a book I had been working on for some time. The book was titled: **How to live for as long as you want, even forever**. I never finished writing that book. I had my greatest revelation instead.

The ancient Greeks admonished us to "Know Thyself". Similarly, Christ told us to look within for something of immense value. Both of these admonitions boil down to the fact that we are oblivious to who we are and what we can be and do. What is buried within us is a secret in the form of a tiny "seed." We must discover this seed and nurture it so it can grow.

What is this secret within?

then the LORD God formed the man of dust from the ground and breathed into his nostrils the breath of life, and the man became a living creature.   Gen 2:7

It is the breath of God.

And what is this breath?

It is of the nature and essence of God.

And what exactly is this nature and essence?

It is Love, Beauty and Joy.

What God breathed into us is our basic soul. It is a packet of consciousness. In its essence, it is love, beauty and joy. This breath is our Holy Spirit that we received initially. It is our one "talent." As stated in the parable of the talents, we are expected to invest our talent and multiply it – doubling what we start with in each life.

What is the fastest way to grow our talent?

If we dwell on love, beauty and joy, adopt and express them in our daily living, then they will grow and blossom.

First, we must accept and love ourselves fully. We are a miracle regardless of our current state.

Second, we must find another and love that individual as ourselves.

Third, we must expand our love to include everyone else.

By loving fully, we know beauty and experience joy.

Becoming love, appreciating beauty and exuding joy, we realize our true nature. We grow our epi-soul. Since our nature is of the nature of God and God is immortal, we realize our immortality.

There is a puzzling passage in The Gospel of Thomas (22):

> *Jesus said to them, "when you make the two into one, and when you make the inner like the outer and the outer like the inner, and the upper like the lower, and when you make the*

> *male and the female into a single one, so that the male will not be male nor the female be female, when you make eyes in place of an eye, a hand in place of a hand, a foot in place of a foot, and an image in place of an image, then you will enter the kingdom."* *

In an earlier passage in the same book, there is this quote:

> *And he said, "Whoever discovers the interpretation of these sayings will not taste death."* *

* The above quotes are from The Gospel of Thomas, part of The Nag Hammadi Scriptures, edited by Marvin Meyer.

Making the two one, is integration – intra, inter and trans integration. *"Making eyes in place of an eye, a hand in place of a hand, a foot in place of a foot, and an image in place of an image"* is walking in another person's shoes, seeing with their eyes, walking with their feet, and in fact becoming and living as them. When we do, we will enter the kingdom of heaven. We will know ourselves and others as love, beauty and joy. We will live as children of God.

This is the secret of the ages. With it, we are powerful, and we can do whatever we set our minds and hearts to. We can live in health, happiness and abundance. We can even decide how long to live and when to depart. Once we decide that it is time to move on, we do so peacefully, gladly and with a knowing smile on our faces.

As we close our eyes and abandon ourselves to sweet sleep and creative dreams, we bid our farewell and say:[1]

> *"Fare you well, people of Orphalese.*
> *This day has ended.*
> *It is closing upon us even as the water-lily upon its own tomorrow.*
> *What was given us here we shall keep,*
> *And if it suffices not, then again must we come together and together stretch our hands unto the giver.*
> *Forget not that I shall come back to you.*
> *A little while, and my longing shall gather dust and foam for another body.*
> *A little while, a moment of rest upon the wind, and another woman shall bear me."*

    Gibran, Khalil. The Prophet. Alfred A. Knopf, New York: 1973

---

[1] Gibran, Khalil. The Prophet. Alfred A. Knopf, New York: 1973

NOTE TO THE READER

This book is an inspired work. It is a labor of love. It is written to empower, enlighten, and set us free. Christ stated, "You will know the truth and the truth will set you free." This book exposes many truths and explains many mysteries.

If you know someone who has lost a loved one or is simply grieving, consider giving them a copy of this book. It will bring solace, comfort and reassure them. This book demystifies and defangs death. It shows that death is not a travesty. It is what we do once we complete our mission.

I sincerely appreciate your help in spreading the word.

With best wishes for peace and enlightenment,

Shahan Shammas

ACKNOWLEDGEMENT

I am grateful to all those who helped make this book a reality. I would like to start with my wife Barbara for her dedicated support, understanding, and patience, and for her reviewing and editing. Barbara's help and support have been invaluable. Next, I would like to thank Olivia Barron, Emily Duttine, and Joseph and Perihan Shammas for their suggestions, encouragement and support.

ABOUT THE AUTHOR

Shahan Shammas

Shahan was born in Aleppo, Syria. At the age of 15, he went to Lebanon where he entered a monastery to study and prepare to be a monk. After two years in the monastery, he left to continue his education. Shahan graduated from the American University of Beirut with a Bachelor's degree in Biology. At the age of 24, Shahan left for the United States, became a US citizen while serving three years in the Army at the medical laboratory of Fort Meade, Md. After working as an Electron Microscopist at the Walter Reed Army Medical Center for 7 years, Shahan started a new career in Information Systems. He worked for the Treasury Department until he retired. After that, Shahan became a teacher at the Judy Hoyer Family Learning Center where he taught Life Skills to adults for ten years. Shahan's background is in the Sciences, Religion, Philosophy and Spirituality. Shahan has lectured extensively in the areas of acquiring knowledge, raising consciousness and actualizing the human potential.

BOOKS BY THIS AUTHOR

Listening To The Voice Within, Becoming Enlightened

What is one "gift" without which we cease to be human? Plants and animals do not have it. Only humans have it. Most do not appreciate this trademark of being human or use it effectively to advance their "Happiness Quotient." In fact, many use it to their detriment. We can learn to use this gift more effectively. It requires us to be fearless, open-minded and intent on improving our lot in life. This gift is Free Will and Freedom of Choice.

Listening to The Voice Within will show us how to best use our Free Will. It is a book that informs, empowers and liberates. It is a guide for transformation. It will help us become enlightened beings. It will push us to grow beyond our comfort zone. To grow, we must break loose of the tethers that constrict and stifle us. Life is a journey, not a destination. If we open our minds and hearts to reason and inspiration and listen to the promptings of The Voice Within, we can be transformed. We need to discover who we are spiritually, instead of what we are materially. Our journey of awakening starts when we

let go of our fears and learn to exercise our freedom of choice. We are responsible for our lives and the decisions we make. This book is full of empowering and liberating insights any one of which has the potential to change lives. Here are some of the topics presented in this book: Who Am I? *Freedom of Choice * Natural Enemies of Humanity * Aging * Life and Death * Raising Our Consciousness * What is Truth? * Journey to Enough * The Second Coming * Love is Power * In God's Image * Good, Bad and Evil * Good News and Sad News * Living in Truth * Self-Examination * The Path Less Travelled * The Transient and the Enduring * Life as an Experiment.
Available at Amazon

A Passion For Living, A Path To Meaning And Joy

Why are we alive? What is the best way to live? Are we the result of an accident of nature? Were we created by God to be tested? Can we have real and satisfying answers to our fundamental questions? I believe so. The key is insistent desire, persistence and a demand to know. "Ask and it will be given to you; seek and you will find; knock and the door will be opened for you." Matt 7:7-8. This is what Christ promised us. These are active verbs. We must take the first steps. Our asking, seeking and knocking, however, must be loud, insistent and persistent until we experience an answer.

To live a life of meaning and joy, we must wake up to who we are. We must live for a purpose that embodies who we want to be. We can be victimized by our circumstances, or we can choose to create the life we want. This is a book about waking up, deciding on something worthwhile to live for, knowing ourselves, deciphering the meaning of life and mastering the art of living. This is a book that explains why we age and die, how to release our brakes, take it easy, do what we can and enjoy ourselves. If we apply the insights in this book, we will discover our passion for living and we will live a life of meaning and joy.

To order A Passion for Living, a path to meaning and joy, for $19.95 plus $3.95 S/H. please email Shahan at shahanshammas@gmail.com

For information about workshops, seminars, and availability for speaking engagements, please email Shahan at shahanshammas@gmail.com

www.ingramcontent.com/pod-product-compliance
Lightning Source LLC
Chambersburg PA
CBHW032106090426
42743CB00007B/252